ARCHIVE
IMAGINING THE EAST END

THE EAST END ARCHIVE AT THE CASS

SUSAN ANDREWS AND NICHOLAS HAEFFNER
EDITED BY ZELDA CHEATLE

CONTENTS

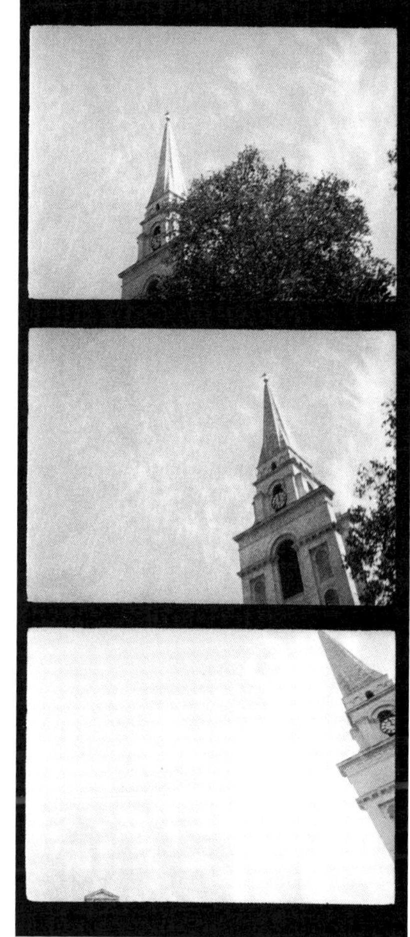

Cover: Susan Andrews, Grace Gents Hair from the series *Up and Down Whitechapel High Street (A11)*, 2009.

Above: Mick Williamson, from the *Photo-Diaries of Mick Williamson*, 1973–2013.

Overleaf: Don McCullin, *Spitalfields Market*, c. 1984.

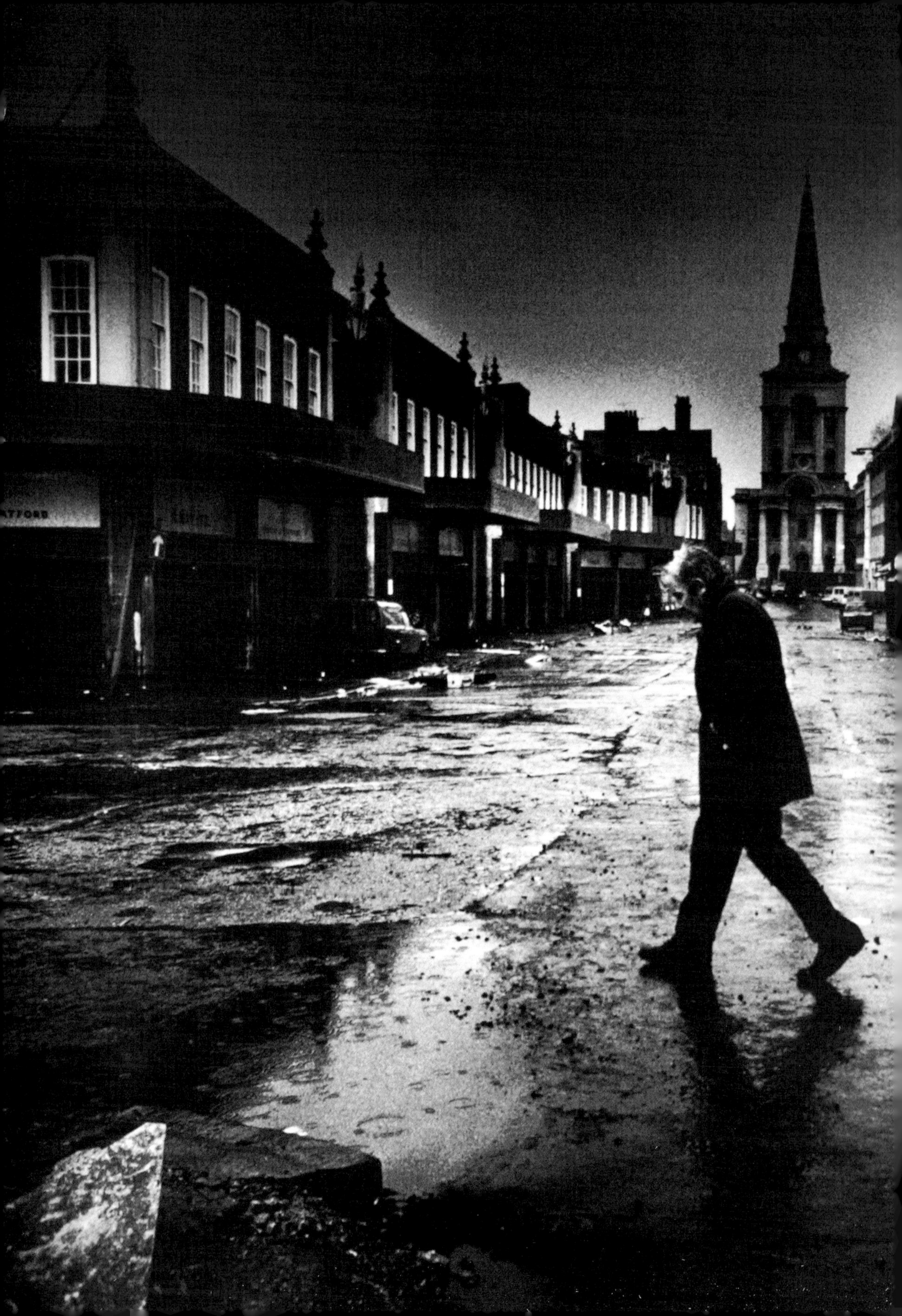

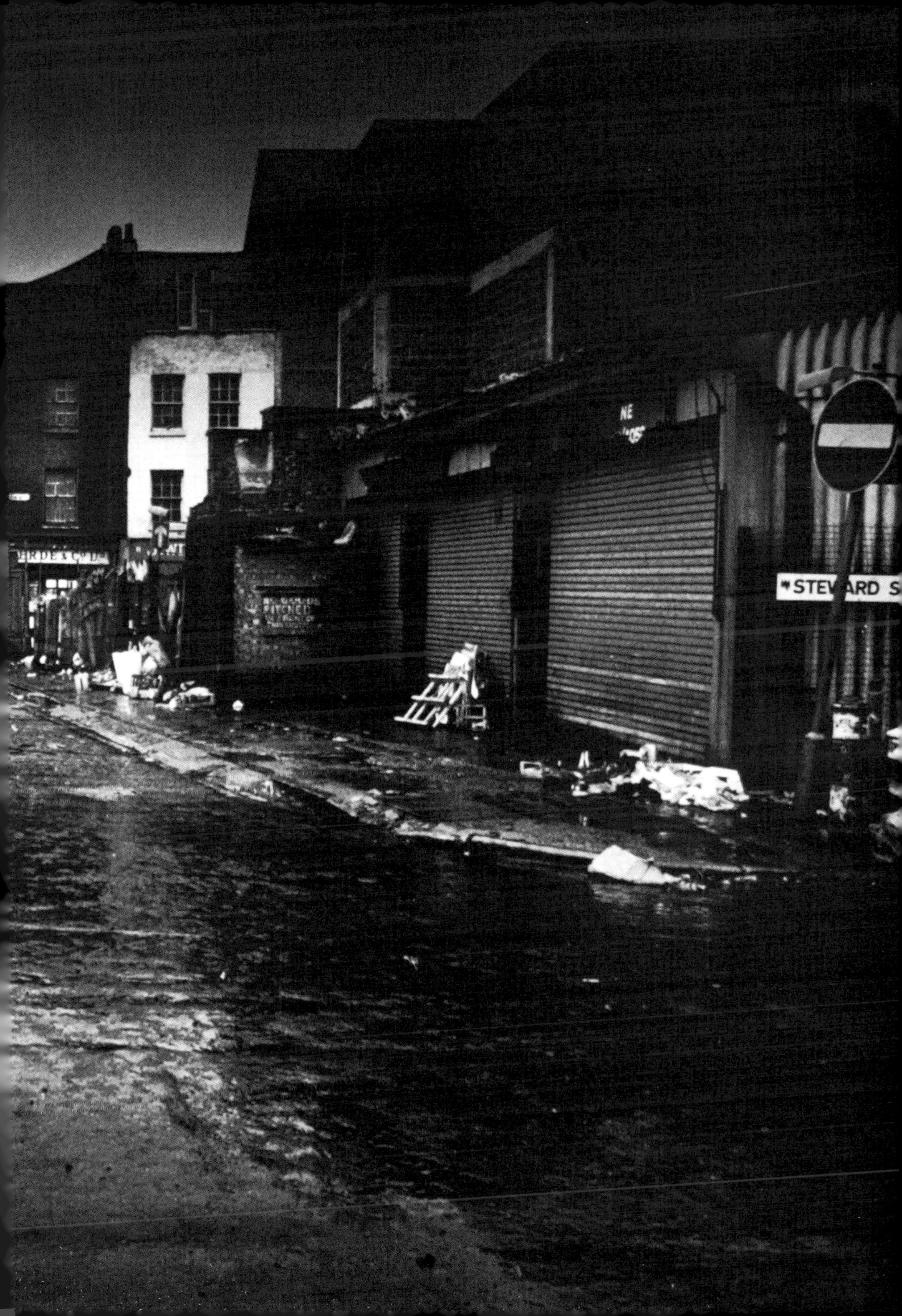
STEWARD S

THE ARCHIVE
SUSAN ANDREWS

With cities, it is as with dreams, everything imaginable can be dreamed but even the most unexpected dream is a rebus that conceals a desire or, its reverse, a fear. Cities, like dreams, are made of desires and fears, even if the thread of their discourse is secret, their rules absurd, their perspectives deceitful, and everything conceals something else.

Italo Calvino, *Invisible Cities*

Architects and urban planners set out to create cities that will both reflect and inspire dreams, combining technology, materials and design to form a contemporary ideological vision. However, despite the best intentions, the city itself engenders an existence beyond the planners' control and the proposed utopias are re-shaped through the unpredictable by-products of invention, creating zones of uncertainty and flux. Such places, which Foucault terms heterotopian, where nothing is fixed and everything is unpredictable and therefore possible, offer up a new space for dreaming.[1] Drawn to the fleeting and with a desire to conserve, these marginal places inspire the photographer to explore the city's secrets.

"Photography and the modern city came of age together. Unlike the small town, where everyone knew everyone, the streets of the city seemed to offer anonymity to those who wanted it, and a constant parade of subjects for those behind the camera."[2] This coincidence of timing has meant that the city's identity has been shaped as much by photographic representation, as by the lived experience. Diverse examples of such varied but influential photographs can be seen throughout the history of photography: Thomas Annan's photographs of the poor in the Glasgow slums that confronted society's conscience; Helen Levitt who photographed New York as a place of neighbourhood and community; Gary Winnogrand whose work depicted social issues of the time; Daido Moriyama's depiction of post-war Japan that reveals aspects of city life as dark and alienating; Martin Parr's unromantic, sometimes cynically humorous observations of the inhabitants of British cities and Steve McClaren's photographs of unusual occurrences and serendipitous juxtapositions on the streets of modern London. These various images feed the imagination and contribute to a complex sense of what the city means.

So it is with London's East End, which constitutes the focus of The East End Archive at The Cass, a place of contradictions, surprises and a rich reserve for the imagination. Indeed, the war photographer Don McCullin, working extensively in the area in the 1960s–1980s commented, "We're sitting in the best reservoir of photographic images that you could ever want for."[3] This same documentary, which is constructed from archive film footage, plugs into much of how we envision the area; a close knit and resilient community fashioned in part by overcrowded conditions and war damage, with proud traditions, thriving markets, the rag trade, the one time hub of international trade in the docklands and a melting pot of immigrant communities. It is a place where many have made a home, including the Chinese, the Irish, French Huguenots, Jewish refugees and Bengalis, each contributing in turn to the thriving and evolving culture that is the East End. However, despite popular affection for East End culture, one cannot forget that life for numerous people over the years has been hard. McCullin maintains, "You cannot walk down Whitechapel without seeing suffering, drama and misery... there are wars that cities have, which I call social wars and I put just as much energy into showing the misery of what I call social wars."[4] This darker history threads further back to a place situated outside the old Roman walls of the City, a story of burials, poverty, violence and racial tension, which weaves through the fabric of its heritage.

Recently, much of the old East End has been (and is still) in the process of being renovated, due in part to the development of the Olympic site at Stratford. Shops and housing along the Olympic route were smartened up and many restored to their original state but, despite all the activity, day-to-day life along the route continued in much the same way as it had done before. However, since the 1980s process of inner city regeneration, the East End has also become home to many more affluent occupants, often eager for riverside accommodation in the old docklands area. This process has not been without its tensions as many of the original East End communities were unable to afford the new homes developed by the London Docklands Development Corporation (LDDC 1981–1997). They felt bitterly let down by the process and squeezed out, relocating to more affordable housing that was less central. In fact, this East End diaspora may have contributed to a shifting sense of the area's boundaries. As the traditional East End population was moved further east due to the process of gentrification, they continued to identify themselves as East Enders because this is what they were.

The East End writer Glinert, on the other hand, remains adamant about what constitutes the East

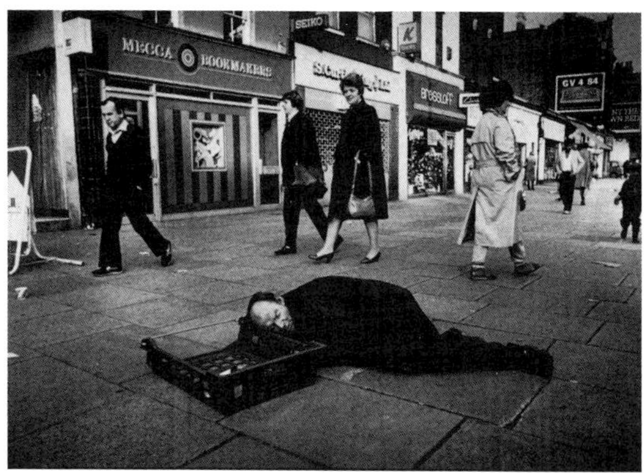

Don McCullin, Whitechapel, c. 1984.

End. "So where is the East End? The East End is that four-mile wide territory east of the City of London leading up to the River Lea, a natural and obvious eastern boundary. The other traditional boundaries are equally formidable: another powerful natural and obvious river boundary—the Thames—to the south, and the thick woodland long prettified into Victoria Park in the North....This is the East End: Bethnal Green, Blackwall, Bow, Bromley-by-Bow, Cubitt Town, Globe Town, Limehouse, Mile End, Millwall, Old Ford, Poplar, Ratcliff, Shadwell, Spitalfields, Stepney, Wapping, Whitechapel."[5] However, some of the new urban developments in the areas outlined above have meant that they ceased to resemble the former East End and its community, despite the geographic location. These places are no longer chaotic and diverse but planned and cohesive. So, despite such certainty expressed by Glinert, "East End" seems to signify more than a fixed location, existing just as much in the imagination as a vivid, cultural space.

A quick search of the Internet reveals a further series of disagreements as to the location of the East End, including discussions about changing postcodes and shifting borough boundaries, revealing that many people are keen to lay claim to the area. One can speculate that this may be due to its fame as a vibrant, chaotic and sometimes dangerous place of journeying and adventure, which has been locked into the imaginations of much of the population; perhaps the East End is simply a more exciting place to be.

Glinert has more to say on the subject: "The term has become ubiquitous in recent years and has come to be too misused in describing anywhere lying roughly between St Paul's Cathedral and the North

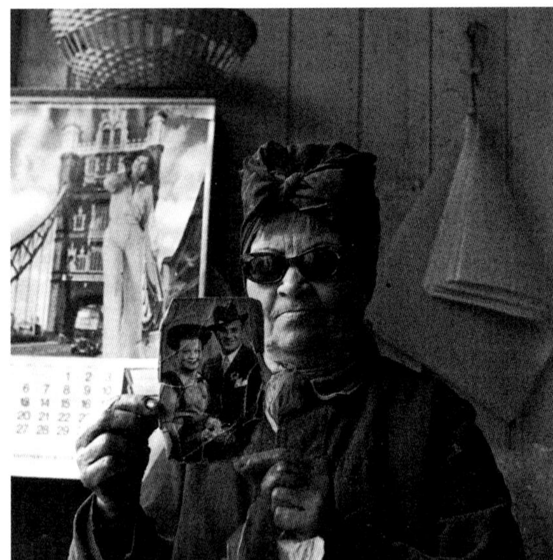

Steven Berkoff, *Jack Waller's Wife*, Leyden Street, 1960s.

Sea. Residents of suburban towns located a short drive from Romford Market or the Lakeside shopping centre in Thurrock lovingly refer to their manor as 'the East End'. Sports commentators on BBC Radio excitedly refer to West Ham United's Boleyn ground in Upton Park 'in the heart of the East End'. Pilots bringing their planes down to land at London City Airport welcome passengers to London's 'famous East End'. Of course, none of these places is in the East End, even though all are to the East of Central London."[6] This broad list of locations suggests hugely diverse communities and certainly seems to reflect a desire to be on the East End map. However, as the cultural historian Alan Palmer points out, the traditional East End sites also had little in common with each other. Indeed, perhaps all of these attempts to classify East End are journalistic constructions, which conceal differences in the face of an assumed identity. "The East End, as a collective concept meriting the use of capital letters, was an invention of the early 1880s. It was created by the London press at a time of falling sales and thwarted political endeavour. Reporters of the previous generation... vividly described particular areas on both sides of the Thames, but recognised differences between Whitechapel, Bethnal Green, Wapping and Limehouse as well as between the Tower Hamlets and Bermondsey or Deptford across the river.... Yet in concentrating on this inner ring of poverty in outer London these writers of the 1880s distorted past and present, giving an artificial unity to old parishes, traditionally distinct from each other."[7]

Above all, it appears that the East End represents diversity and change; its location is not fixed and is hard to pin down. Maybe, as David Howells suggests, the East End is "a territory perpetually in need of transformation, vicious and semi-criminal, a dark continent off-limits to all but the most intrepid missionaries and pioneers... 'East End' is in reality a state of mind, the necessary frontier of 'regeneration' wherever that may be."[8]

The East End Archive at The Cass reflects and embodies these ideas and inconsistencies. It is currently being developed by an inter-disciplinary team within the School of Art as an online "archive for the future" that represents not only history as it was lived and imagined but also the role of photography in contributing to an understanding of the times. As such, it is as much about photography as about history. The archive therefore collects a broad range of bodies of photographic work, which are related to the East End. These collections give context to the work offering a means of understanding the photographers' practice, their working methods, intentions and obsessions. In so doing it is possible to recognise the relationship between history and the means of recording, for the historian to unpick the visual document and identify its reliability and for the artist to consider the process of documentation and its relationship with its subject. Moreover, by giving the photographs context through holding the body of work some of the concerns raised by Alan Sekula regarding archives may be addressed. Sekula claimed that archives constitute "a territory of images" and that "the possibility of meaning is 'liberated' from the actual contingencies of use. But this liberation is also a loss, an abstraction from the complexity and richness of use, a loss of context."[9] In consideration of such issues, The East End Archive at The Cass has constructed a framework that aims to give context and meaning to the images by situating them within each photographer's practice.

Additionally, The Sir John Cass Faculty of Art, Architecture and Design, which hosts The East End Archive, has a long history in the area and was founded by the Sir John Cass Foundation in 1899 as The Sir John Cass Technical Institute. Although its name has changed on several occasions reflecting political and historic shifts in 'ownership', it remains synonymous with art and the creative industries and the link with the Sir John Cass Foundation continues to the present day. The philanthropist Sir John Cass (1661–1718) is himself buried in the local churchyard of St Mary Matfelon, now Altab Ali Park, which lies adjacent to The Cass and diagonally opposite the Whitechapel Gallery. This location on the border of the City and East End has been a source of engagement and inspiration for The Cass and for the many locals and foreigners who encounter its contradictions. It is from this rich resource that the archive draws its photographic collections where the contributors all have close connections with the area either through work, home or by desire, which is often coupled with a strong sense of ownership—it is 'our' East End.

The East End Archive at The Cass also exists on another frontier, as a virtual rather than physical artefact, representing unpredictable, unknown territory, rife with possibilities and potential traps. Although at face value the virtual world offers the ideal solution to the pressures of diminishing space, whilst also presenting opportunities for unlimited public access to the collections, it hides a range of questions and problems. As Pablo Ruiz Garcia notes "the new digital world is subject to constant instability because of the extremely rapid evolution of the technology. This evolution presents two faces of the same coin: one side creates uncertainties and the other creates new opportunities."[10]

Garcia elaborates on some of the essential issues pertinent to online collections, in particular those relating to metadata, "Unlike all previous collections, there is something uniquely different about a digital archive: it is virtual, nothing more than machine-readable code. For this reason, to ensure that the code will still be readable in future, detailed information about the technology used to make the digital capture itself must be passed on. Some of this information—metadata—is embedded automatically into the image file during capture. Other metadata about the quality of the capture system must be determined by technical tests and inputted manually. Given that computer search engines use metadata to identify and locate images, the importance of metadata in this field cannot be overstated."[11] These considerations reveal a level of anxiety regarding digital image conservation due to the newness of the technologies and procedures, and an inability to predict how technology may advance.

However, beyond issues of image management, concerns relating to the virtual photograph extend to other aspects of conservation. The ease with which future generations of archivists, who deeming something unimportant may irretrievably delete images, means that an archive that misrepresents the original concerns of the photographers is a real possibility. Other related questions arise such as, "what did the printed work actually look like in terms of colour, quality and scale?" Some of these factors may be partially addressed through image management systems, but as already stated the technology is changing so quickly that these may be difficult to track and notes relating to other qualities may be too subjective for someone else to properly evaluate.

With some of these questions in mind, Graham Diprose and Mike Seaborne have embarked on an ambitious research project to which The East End Archive is contributing. Their paper "An Alternative approach to Archiving Digital Images into the 23rd Century" addresses a method of archiving using small scale prints that may be re-copied for exhibition with limited loss of original quality which would be held in addition to the online files. Archiving in this way would require much less space than conventional methods and whole collections of digital images may be held with actual references to the photographer's edit and the way in which work was intended to be seen.

Seaborne and Diprose summarise some of the concerns that lead to the research project as follows: "Many museums and archives worldwide are taking every opportunity to digitise their collections, both to facilitate a much wider access online and to reduce the need to handle the originals. However, it does not follow that the digitised data files will survive any longer than the artefacts that have been copied nor, in the case of digitally-born images, is there any guarantee that these image files will continue to be accessible or readable in the long term as equipment becomes obsolete and file formats change. No one can predict how often digital image data will need to be migrated from one generation of file format, or file storage system, to another. Neither can we predict the future costs involved, nor the amount of storage that will need to be available, nor the risks from technical mishaps, 'bit rot' or human error."[12]

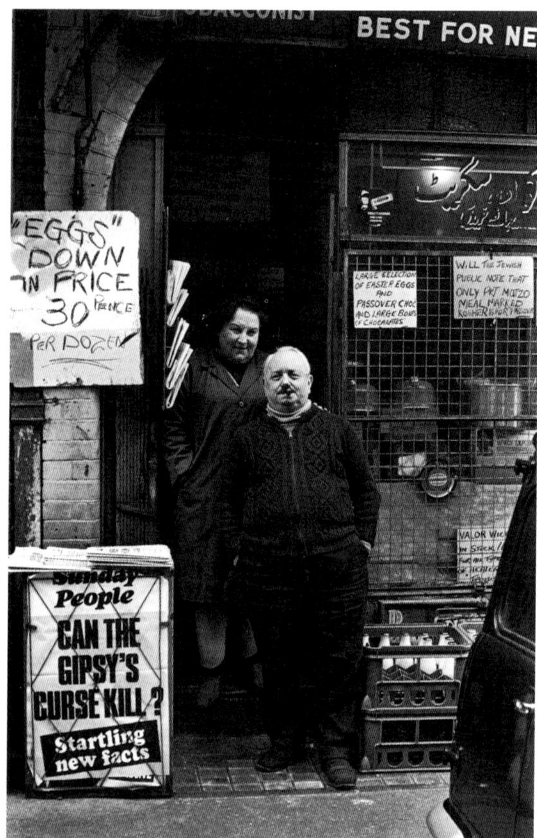

Steven Berkoff, Stepney, 1960s.

The costs of digitisation and management may indeed be significant particularly for smaller archives. Environmental Images (developed as a strand of the original Environmental Picture Library which was sold to Greenpeace), was forced to close in 2001 despite the timely nature of its content, as it was unable to afford the many digital developments that rapidly occurred. They simply did not have the resources to stay abreast of the trends.

Diprose and Seaborne suggest that versions of archived files saved as small prints may be both space and cost effective, acting as an insurance against unforeseen technological accidents and developments. "We therefore propose an alternative approach to the archiving of vital images and documents as hard copy prints made with pigment inks on archival quality paper. Prints may be read without any technological interface and archivists have had centuries of experience in the long-term preservation of documents and images on paper. We suggest that archiving images as pigment prints will increase their chances of survival into the twenty-third century and that this format is relatively easy and inexpensive to achieve in comparison to other digital preservation strategies. We are not advocating this method as a replacement for digital storage and data migration but rather as a very sound form of insurance, one based on well-proven paper conservation methods."

This process may indeed alleviate many of the anxieties surrounding digital conservation. With limited space one could still store an accurate and relatively stable photograph whilst benefiting from the ease of public access and dissemination that relates to digital archives. Interested in the potential of the process, The East End Archive at The Cass has embarked on a pilot study with Diprose and Seaborne to explore the capability of such techniques. "The aim of the pilot project being undertaken in partnership with the East End Archive is to establish the working parameters involved in printing a broad selection of digitally-born and digitised photographic images. In particular, we aim to establish the optimum print sizes for archiving, taking into account the nature of the images themselves, the costs of making and storing different sizes of prints and the levels of image quality acceptable for different purposes."[13]

Beyond the problematic territory of digital conservation, the biggest perceived benefit of online archiving must be for the worldwide access that is given to the public, although there may still be some question as to its universality. However, the virtual nature of The East End Archive at The Cass also means that the archivists' relationship with the material is altered. Photographers maintain full control over their copyright and deposit small digital files for online viewing with some larger files for photographic reproduction for exhibitions. The East End Archive has no exclusive rights over image use and will always ask permission to use images for any purpose. In this way, rather than having ownership of the deposits, the archive team is caretaker and facilitator, curating a collection of photographic practice that relates to the East End, in order to create a resource for research, education, public engagement and debate.

Furthermore, the Archive's existence within The Cass offers another distinctive opportunity in terms of how it might be developed. Unlike museums and other official institutions our agenda is less rigid and we can grow the collections in a more organic fashion. The first contributors had internal or very close links with The Cass but gradually the photographers are coming from a broader base that shares a common interest in photography, the East End and the potential of online archives.

The East End Archive at The Cass addresses the photographer's relationship with the world and it is our belief that valuable photography comes from this engagement, rather than being a simple feature of mechanical reproduction. Paul Graham reflecting on his photographic practice has said, "It was worth it, because it is something real, that didn't exist before you made it exist: a sentient work of art and power and sensitivity, that speaks of this world and your fellow human beings place within it. Isn't that beautiful?"[14]

Archive: Imagining the East End includes selections of photographs from the personal archives of photographers who are represented in The East End Archive at The Cass, as well as the work of other local groups with whom there are links, such as The Building Exploratory's *Panorama High Street East 2012*. The book introduces some of the central themes and considerations specific to building an online "archive for the future" and it is important to understand that in constructing this archive, the East End is seen as a contested and conceptual space, rather than a specific geographic location. Additionally, the bodies of photographic work, together with written statements and evaluations, offer a broader context for rigorous engagement with issues of photographic representation and the construction of narratives. Finally, an argument is made for the expanded conception of a photographic archive, seen not simply as a repository of 'factual' documents but rather a place where myth, memory, and fantasy may intermingle.

1. The term "heterotopia" was used in a 1967 in an unpublished lecture, "On Other Species".
2. Warner Marien, Mary, *100 Ideas that Changed Photography*, London: Laurence King Publishing, 2012, p. 169.
3. *London on Film—The East End*, BBC4, 2012.
4. *London on Film.*
5. Glinert, Ed, *East End Chronicles*, London: Penguin Books, 2005, p. x.
6. Glinert, *East End Chronicles*, p. ix.
7. Palmer, A, *The East End: Four Centuries of London Life*, London: John Murray, 2000, p. 85.
8. Howells, David, *Activate 4*, London: Sir John Cass School of Art, 2007, p. 8.
9. Wells, Liz, ed., "Reading an Archive: Photography between Labour and Capital" by Allan Sekula, *The Photography Reader*, Abingdon: Routledge, 2003, p. 444.
10. Garcia, Pablo Ruiz, "Digitizing Photography Collections—key points", *Activate 3*, London: Sir John Cass School of Art, 2006, p. 4.
11. Garcia, "Digitizing Photography", p. 4.
12. Diprose, Graham, and Seaborne, Mike, "An Alternative Approach to Conserving Digital Images into the 23rd Century", http://ewic.bcs.org/upload/pdf/ewic_ev11_s7paper4.pdf, 2012.
13. Diprose and Seaborne, "An Alternative Approach".
14. Graham, Paul, "We Belong Together", *MFA Photography, graduation book introduction*, Yale: 2009.

THE ARCHIVAL TURN

NICHOLAS HAEFFNER

What images might run through our minds when we hear of an archive of East End photography? Archives are traditionally seen as repositories for documents. A great many photographs of the East End are in the documentary mode. From John Galt's Victorian explorations into that 'dark continent', to the recently published book *East End Photographs* taken by the actor Steven Berkoff, East End photography has tended to be synonymous with documentary photography.[1] An archive of East End photography might therefore be assumed to consist of documentary images and to have the status of documentary evidence. However, in what follows I hope to show that few things are as straightforward as documentary realism, especially where the East End is its notional subject matter. Instead of clinging to a purist notion of 'how it really was', I shall argue that the East End archive is at its most interesting when a long tradition of documentary style photography meets what has become known as an 'archival turn' in contemporary art practice, which mixes fictional with documentary modes.

Photographic images of the East End have long been bound up with various forms of advocacy, especially campaigns for social reform on behalf of various groups including The London City Mission (an organisation dedicated to the promotion of Christianity in the East End) and the Workers Suffrage Federation (a feminist group which aimed to further the rights of working class women). Documentary style photography in the East End played an important role in each group's activities. For instance, The Bedford Institute Association, a Quaker charity, produced a yearbook detailing their activities, using photographs to promote their particular form of Christian charity. In the promotional material, children play a key role as figures for empathy but also as 'raw material' to be worked on.

Documentary photographs are bound up with reformist discourse which has taken a stand on a range of issues and has been closely associated with both politics and religion. Many photographic projects acted as a challenge to negative and

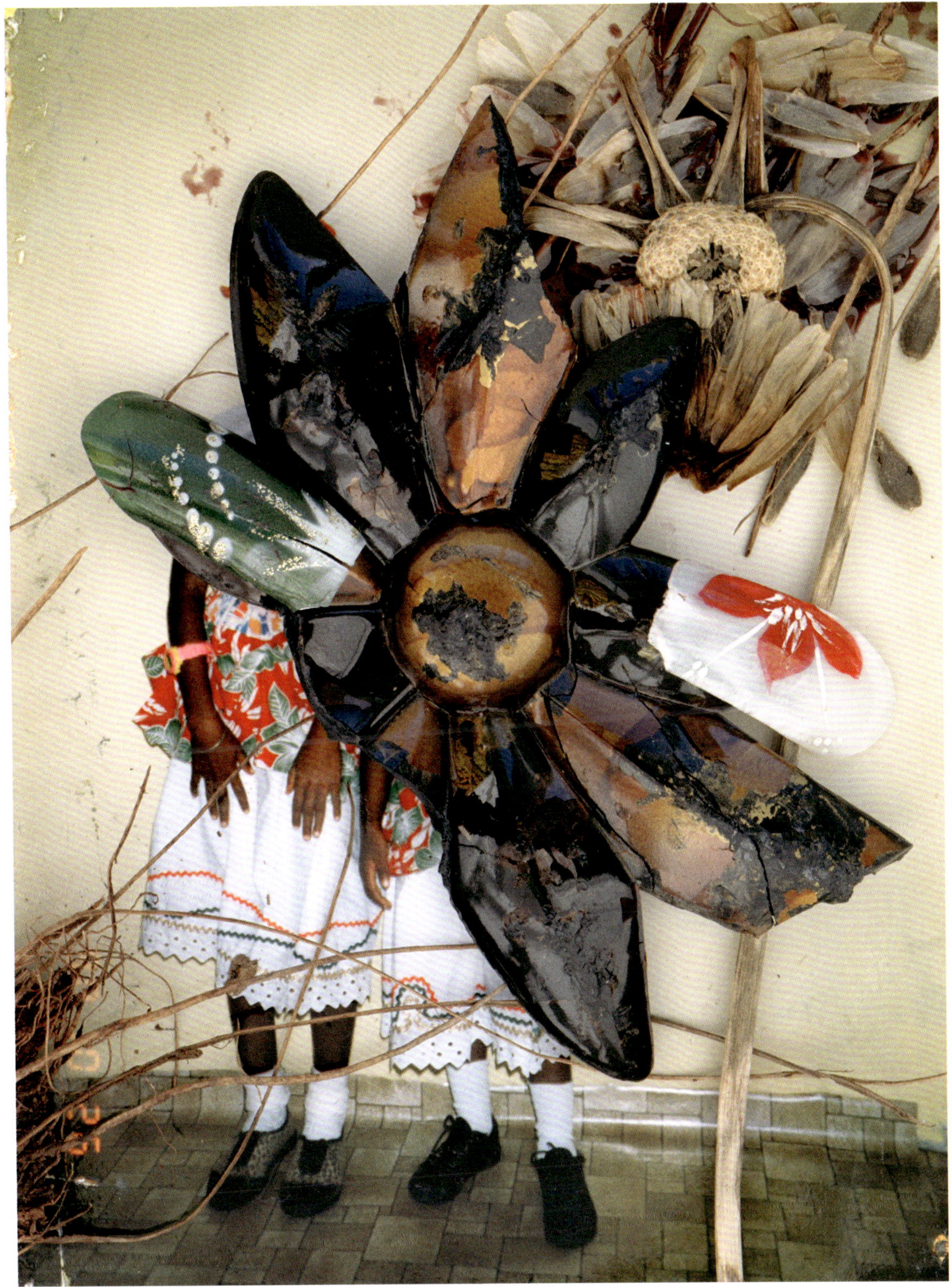

Stephen Gill, Extract from *Hackney Flowers*, Hackney, 2007.

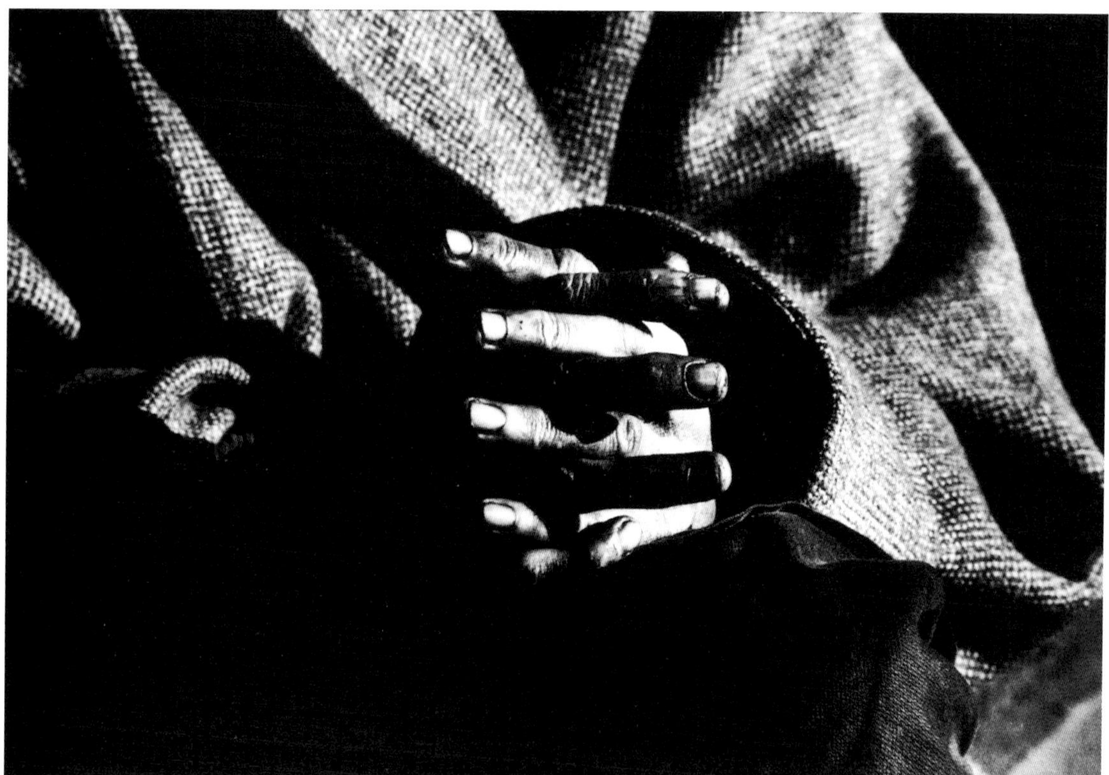

Don McCullin, *The Hands of Jean*, Brick Lane, c. 1984.

stereotypical preconceptions about the East End which imagined it as a place of vice and degeneracy. To counter such prejudices, many documentary photographers began to advocate for a more sympathetic portrayal of the East End, a notable example being the work of Cyril Arapoff for the magazine *Picture Post*.

The links between photographing the East End and such forms of advocacy has become so strong that the very idea of an archive of East End photography is likely to raise suspicions of yet more middle class 'do-goodery'. In addition, there has arisen a powerful scepticism concerning the neutrality, truthfulness and straightforwardness of documentary photography. In 1877, the photographer John Thompson and the journalist Adolphe Smith could present their East End photography as a simple factual record: "And now we also have sought to portray these harder phases of life, bringing to bear the precision of photography in illustration of our subject. The unquestionable accuracy of this testimony will enable us to present true types of the London Poor and shield us from the accusation of either underrating or exaggerating individual peculiarities of appearance."[2]

In the face of such assertions of photographic innocence, Mike Seaborne insists that East End documentary photography has always been a rhetorical device: never neutral, always working in support of one ideological discourse or another.[3] Furthermore, the apparent popularity of the East End as a location for documentary photography conceals a darker history of constant surveillance and attempts at control of an area constantly stigmatised as politically unstable, unruly, disordered and likely to infect the rest of the body politic with its radical ideas. It is also important to note that certain images associated with poverty have become something of a fetish. Indeed, in what must be one of the first such archives, the photographer Arthur J Munby (1828–1910) made thousands of images of labouring women, some of whom were dirtied for the camera. Judging from the patterns of repetition in the series, pit girls were a particular favourite.[4] Don McCullin's East End work is categorised as documentary photography or reportage yet his own account of his work suggests something rather more than recording or reporting. In a lengthy self-penned essay included in his book *Homecoming*, 1979, McCullin says that photography for him is "like an illness" and "a bad dream". McCullin foregrounds his aesthetic interest in the subjects of his photographs and says "I feel guilty because they've been taken with the eye of a photographer not the concern of a social worker... the only two ingredients I think are worthwhile are mood and drama."[5]

Yet for the most part, images of the East End poor have played on a core nineteenth century idea of 'sympathy', linked in reformist discourse to morality. Sympathy was made possible by the imagination (also known in the nineteenth century as 'fancy', an image caused by the mind). In his *Theory of Moral Sentiments*, first published in 1759, Adam Smith wrote that the source of our fellow feeling for the misery of others is mobilised by "changing places in fancy with the sufferer".[6] Today, Adam Smith is best known for his later work, *The Wealth of Nations*, upon which much free market economics is based. However, the link between economics and morality remains, in an inverted version of Smith's insistence on the importance of sympathy. At the time of writing, opinion poll research shows that a substantial proportion of the public endorse a harder hearted view of the poor than we have seen since the end of the Second World War. Such a view seems, in an uncanny return to Victorian moralising about the East End, to presume that poverty is some sort of lifestyle option, favoured by the lazy, immoral and feckless.

In subtitling this photographic collection "Imagining the East End", some ghosts of Adam Smith's influential theory of morality may still echo. Yet the fortunes of the term 'imagination' have not been so good in recent times. The liberal humanistic idea of 'empathy' (imagining ourselves in others' shoes) has been the subject of a programmatic critique from deconstruction which casts otherness and difference as irreducible, unknowable and always liable to be appropriated by others for dubious ends. In another influential attack, Walter Benjamin describes the empathy of the historian as an "indolence of the heart... which despairs of grasping and holding the genuine historical image as it flares up briefly".[7]

Unquestionably, to pretend that you can easily put yourself in the shoes of a poverty-stricken East Ender if you are a comfortably off intellectual is problematic. To do the same as an archivist, trying to imagine how the past was for distant others is equally problematic. During the 1990s, t-shirts were sold with slogans such as "it's a gay thing, you wouldn't understand" or "it's a black thing, you wouldn't understand" as a reaction against this kind of liberal solidarity with the downtrodden or marginalised. Imagination also has a tendency to abstract its visions from the nitty gritty (and often boring) world of economics and politics. However vivid our imagination, it will always get it wrong if these grinding determinants are not sufficiently acknowledged.

The privileging of imagination has, perhaps paradoxically, been accompanied by a veneration for social realism (this is, after all, a society which can produce *Dr Who* and the films of Ken Loach, claiming both as quintessentially British). This enthusiasm for social realism is rooted in the perceived truth of the photographic document. But since the 1970s, various forms of deconstruction have whittled away at the very idea of realism, which can be viewed as simply a convention.

For instance, images of poor East End children playing in the streets and smiling are among the durable images of twentieth century East End photography. Perhaps this is because they tend to position the spectator as caring and concerned (based on what could be called the Dickensian morality—the poor are simple and virtuous, the rich are sophisticated, corrupt and exploitative but the spectator, usually comfortably off, is nonetheless exempt from judgement). The image overleaf, features a photograph taken in Spitalfields in 1912 by Horace Warner. It was reprinted on the top of a box for charitable donations for the Bedford Institute, a philanthropic organisation promoting "religious and social work". Such images are not merely conventions, but ideological seductions. This particular convention (child poverty as charming pathos) helps to ground the more general accusation that documentary realism is merely a repertoire of

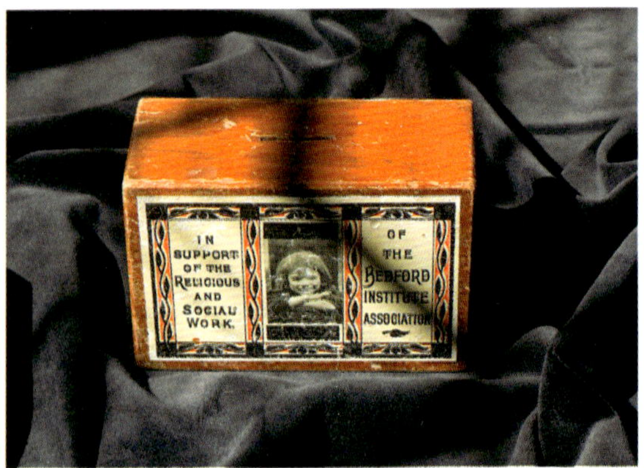

Nicholas Haeffner, Donation Box with photo by Horace Warner, 2013.

well worn tropes, usually chosen because of their tried and tested ability to create the desired effect in the viewer. Rather than being *sui generis*, the argument goes, realism is just one fictional genre among others: "we move merely among different, competing genres of fiction making, of which realism is just the most confused, and perhaps the most obtuse because the least self-conscious about its own procedures".[8] All this can quickly lead to a sceptical view of the archive, no longer a hallowed repository of human civilisation where the public can access the truth but rather "a place of repressions and supressions". [9]

However, even if a degree of skepticism is healthy, it is possible to defend the documentary or realist impulse against the charges that it is merely the use of conventions to produce a 'realistic effect'. As Wood argues, "the point to make about convention is not that it is untruthful *per se* but that it has a way of becoming, by repetition steadily more and more conventional".[10]

Even if we accept the charge that at least some photographers engaged in the unreflective repetition of conventions (or, in more loaded language, stereotyping), things are not straight-forward. The fact that appeals to realism are mixed up with the use of realist conventions (or even stereotypes), need not in itself be a fatal objection to documentary photography dealing with the East End.

Certainly William Fishman's *The Streets of East London*, with its chapter headings of "poverty", "philanthropy", "crime", "immigrants" and "radicals" might seem to fit the notion that a somewhat rigid and highly conventional grid has been placed over "the blooming, buzzing confusion" of reality that is the living East End.[11] A rich tradition of religious and mystical thinking is certainly missing from this list. As Ed Glinert notes "the area has long been prone to spiritual and mystical excess" (with Kabbalism a popular belief, and Masonic ritual part of the key to the Ripper murders).[12]

However, it may be necessary to accept that, over time, work that once offered a fresh and challenging perspective on poverty and deprivation for instance, may lose its ability to shake its audience out of its habits of mind. The shock of the new needs to be continuously re-enacted and it is the role of the artist to refresh and reinvigorate the languages of representation so that the world can be estranged for us each time we assume that we have it mapped out as a stable entity.

The new millennium has seen the onset of the archival turn in contemporary art. The idea that documentation is a form of contemporary art had already been anticipated in the 1930s when John Grierson, the founder of the British Documentary Movement, defined documentary as "the creative treatment of actuality". Grierson hired Modernists such as Len Lye, Humphrey Jennings and Alberto Cavalcanti to direct documentaries in which the artist was encouraged to creatively re-invent the genre with each film. In Grierson's eyes, "There need be no tension between documentary and art... 'the fact of the matter' could be a path to modern beauty."[13]

Many contemporary artists such as Tacita Dean, the Otolith Group, Felix Gonzalez-Torres, Zoe Leonard and Thomas Ruff have taken the archival turn, producing works in which documentary practices and materials are used in highly unorthodox ways. The film *Handsworth Songs*, 1986, made by Black Audio Film Collective, mixes family photographs, newsreel footage and poetry to create an hallucinatory autopsy on the uprisings in Birmingham in 1985.

There is also a substantial body of theoretical commentary on the archival turn.[14] Much recent photographic work is also inspired by the writings of Foucault (1969/2002) and Derrida (1995/1998).[15]

The work of the Lebanese artist Walid Raad is worth noting here for its theoretical grounding and refusal to accept a stable distinction between factual and fictional photography. Raad created the Atlas Group in 1999, which is not a group at all but rather a fictional entity and a figment of his imagination. Raad's work concerns Lebanese history, in particular, the Lebanese wars between 1975 and 1991. His exhibition Miraculous Beginnings at the Whitechapel Gallery in 2011 was accompanied by a set of questions which frame his artistic inquiry: "What is a photographic image? What type of record does it provide? Can a photograph ever tell the truth or just provide a semblance of reality? How is history constructed, and how the history of art?"[16] The exhibition itself consisted of a series of photographic images, apparently documents of war torn Lebanon, some of which are credited to Souheil Bachar who, we are told, was held hostage for ten years and Dr Fadl Fakhouri who took a photograph every time he thought the war had ended. Further engagement with the project, however, reveals that these two characters, along with many of the images, are fictions of Raad's imagination, leading one critic to compare Raad to "a successful magician" creating an aura of "illusion/delusion": "Raad not only occupies the disputed borderline between reportage and art he manipulates it, mixing fact and fiction and trying to decipher those points at which memories are either suppressed or become state policy.[17] Raad's approach exemplifies the transition 'from the archive as repository of documents to the archive as a dynamic and generative production tool'".[18]

Concurrent with the archival turn there has been a notable tendency for some photographic artists to blur the boundaries between fiction and documentary, a move in some ways foreshadowed in the 1990s by fashion photographers such as Jason Edwards and Elaine Constantine (the latter strongly influenced by Chris Killip's downbeat images of the northeast of England). Cristina de Middel, nominated for the Deutsche Bourse prize for her fictional photobook *The Afronauts*, began her career as a photojournalist and saw the project as a way of combating stereotypical views of Africa in the news media.

The art critic Michael Newman, while noting that the documentary photograph and the snapshot have been associated with evidence and witness, points to an emerging space for the photograph between cinema and painting, which, while it may be based on literary and documentary sources, is nevertheless also preoccupied with *mise-en-scène*. Jeff Wall's work is exemplary of this approach to photography. Newman notes that "drawing on models of painting and cinematography allowed Wall to explore dimensions specific to photography including its peculiar construction of space, its temporality such as the fixing of the momentary, and the credulity on the part of the viewer that it arouses".[19] Wall himself has argued that, even if it has a relationship to the event, the narrative, the account and the chronicle, "a photograph cannot fundamentally be an account". Wall distinguishes his work from documentary photography which aims to be the equivalent of journalistic prose and instead aims to be more like a "prose poem".[20] Jeff Wall's work has been an important influence on the Hackney based photographer Tom Hunter. Hunter's work uses elements of fiction through his preference for staged scenes most evident in his partial recreation of old master paintings by Vermeer and the Pre-Raphaelites. Yet his series *Living in Hell* is also based on newspaper headlines from his local paper *The Hackney Gazette*. Hunter is unabashed about calling himself an artist, noting that "there are a lot of photographers who are scared of the word 'art' or 'artist' and have taken up photography because it doesn't have those pretentious connotations. There is an idea that art is un-masculine." [21]

Another Hackney based artist, Stephen Gill, has staged a series of spectacular collisions between documenting the area in which he lives and wild flights of fancy. In his photobook *Hackney Flowers*, people and places are suddenly, inexplicably overwhelmed by flowers.[22]

In their insistence that the photograph is at the same time imaginative encounter and document, Hunter and Gill are exemplary of the kind of work which the curators of the East End Archive believe will open up new horizons of possibility in relation to the archival impulse.

The East End Archive at The Cass is not there to reify images and concepts but to open them out to new interpretations. An archive of this kind is less like a filing cabinet or a collection of dusty old boxes and more like a cabinet of curiosities. Accordingly, this book is not an exhibition catalogue but a critical compilation which works through montage to deconstruct some of the received notions of what an archive is, where the East End is and what documentary photography is all about.

Opposite: Tom Hunter, *The Art of Squatting,* Hackney, 1997.

1. For the use of the term "dark continent" in this context see Schwarz, Bill, "Where Horses Shit, a Thousand Sparrows Feed" in John Corner and Sylvia Harvey, *Enterprise and Heritage: Crosscurrents of the National Culture*, London: Routledge.
2. Thompson, John and Adolphe Smith, *Victorian London Street Life in Historic Photographs*, New York: Dover, 1877/1994, p. 1.
3. Seaborne, Mike, *Photography and the East End of London 1900–1939: An Examination of the Work of Three Photographers*, unpublished MA thesis, 1995.
4. Williams, Val and Susan Bright, *How We Are: Photographing Britain* London: Tate, 2007, p. 12.
5. McCullin, Don, *Homecoming*, London: Macmillan, 1979, p. 190.
6. Smith, Adam, *The Theory of Moral Sentiments*, Indianapolis: Liberty Fund, 1982, p. 48.
7. Benjamin, Walter, *Illuminations*, London: Pimlico, 1999, p. 256.
8. Wood, James, *How Fiction Works*, New York: Vintage, 2009, p. 171.
9. Derrida, Jacques, *Archive Fever*, Chicago: University of Chicago Press, 1998.
10. Wood, *How Fiction Works*, p. 178.
11. James, William, *Principles of Psychology*, Cambridge, MA: Harvard University Press, 1880/1991, p. 462 and William J Fishman, *Streets of East London*, London: Five Leaves, 2006.
12. Glinert, Ed, *East End Chronicles*, Harmondsworth: Penguin, 2005.
13. John Grierson in Julian Stallabrass, *Documentary*, London: Whitechapel, 2013, p. 12.
14. Enwezor, O, and W Hartshorn, *Archive Fever: uses of the document in contemporary art*, London: Steidl, 2008; Osthoff, Simone, *Performing the Archive: The Transformation of the Archive in Contemporary Art from Repository of Documents to Art Medium*, New York: Atropos Press, 2009, and Merewether, Charles, *The Archive* , London: Whitechapel 2006.
15. Foucault, Michel, *The Archaeology of Knowledge*, London: Routledge, 2002.
16. Whitechapel Gallery, *Walid Raad: Miraculous Beginnings*, http://www.whitechapelgallery.org/shop/product/category_id/42/product_id/777, accessed 2 July 2013.
17. Istim, B, 2013, *Review of Miraculous Beginnings*, http://thecollectivereview.com/brigitte-istim/walid-raads-miraculous-beginnings.html, accessed 2 July 2013.
18. Osthoff, p. 11.
19. Newman, Michael, *Jeff Wall: Works and Collected Writings*, Barcelona: Ediciones Poligrafa, 2007, p. 9.
20. Newman, *Jeff Wall*, p.12.
21. Hunter, T, Interview with Katy Barron, 2013, http://www.tomhunter.org/tom-hunter-interviewed-by-katy-barron, accessed 9 July 2013.

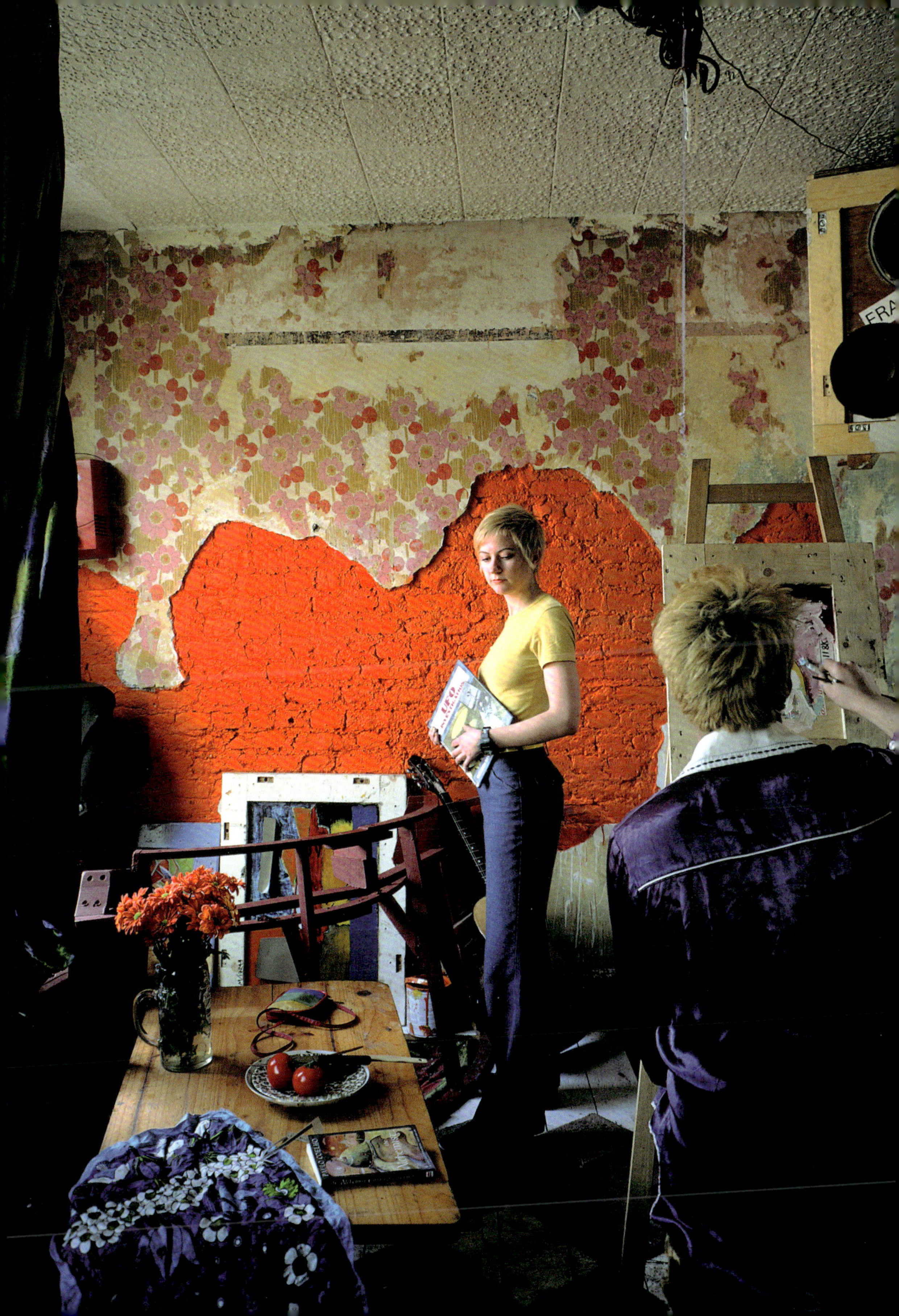

WHY ONE IS NEVER ENOUGH

SUSAN ANDREWS

But if it's everywhere and all the time, and so easy to make, then what's of value? Which pictures matter? Is it the hard won photograph, knowing, controlled, pre-visualised? Yes. Or are those contrived, dry and belaboured? Sometimes. Is it the offhand snapshot made on a whim. For sure. Or is that just a lucky observation, some random moment caught by chance? Maybe. Is it an intuitive expression of liquid intelligence? Exactly. Or the distillation of years of looking seeing thinking photography. Definitely.

Paul Graham

Photographers are collectors. In the most immediate way, they are collectors of fractions of seconds that have been stolen from time and frozen. Of course, many of these stolen moments can be rediscovered on walls, in books, in family albums, and nowadays on the many photo-sharing websites. However, since its invention, photography has also been used more systematically as a recording mechanism to document collections and verify objects, places, people and events. This is because "a photograph passes for incontrovertible truth that a given thing happened. The picture may distort: but there is always a presumption that something exists, or did exist."[1]

Anna Atkins was one of the first photographers to systematically record collected objects, using the "photogenic drawing" technique where an object was placed on light sensitive paper that was then exposed to the sun. In 1843 she published the first book to be illustrated with photographic images, *Photographs of British Algae: Cyanotype Impressions*. This body of work represents both her personal interests and the photographic technology that was available at the time, but it also embodies the Victorian obsession with collection and typology. We can understand when viewing the work that the messages we receive from looking extend beyond the visual reference, a trace of white marked in a sea of blue. We recognise that the photograph imparts as much about personal interest and cultural context as it does about the object itself.

Viewed retrospectively, the broader interpretation of the work is easy to see in a way that may not be as apparent when considering the modern photographic medium with which we are so familiar, as its place is so interwoven with everyday experience. In fact, the photographic subject is always mediated by a variety of factors such as photographic technology, subjective intention and interest, and cultural and personal context. Understanding this is key to decoding photographic meaning and all discussions on the subject. As Maholy-Nagy famously remarked: "A knowledge of photography is just as important as that of the alphabet. The illiterate of the future will be ignorant of the use of camera and pen alike."[2]

From the early days of its development, photography quickly became known as an art form for everyone, as it was concerned with a variety of subjects and appeared to offer the potential for the democratic education of those who did not otherwise have the means to access knowledge.[3] The medium's "indisputable accuracy" and a conviction that photographs did not need interpretation by scholars or experts, "to see is to know" reinforced this belief.[4] Furthermore, Louis Daguerre, inventor of the Daguerreotype in the 1830s, commented that the photographic medium would allow people to "form collections of all kinds" and that these collections could educate the masses.[5] In fact, few actually managed to methodically collect photographs and for most people the practice of photography was limited to the family album, which itself conformed to a formulaic set of conventions. Indeed, it wasn't until the retrospective photography exhibition at MoMA, Photography 1839–1937, curated by Beaumont Newhall, that the medium had the first showing that reflected seriously on its qualities.

However, a group of people had emerged in the 1880s intent on collecting photographs. Known as The Record and Survey Tradition, it was made up of interested amateurs who had joined photographic societies after the introduction of the gelatin dry plate and the new hand-held cameras. They saw themselves as record-makers for the historians of the future, usually donating the work to a local museum or public library. These photographers distanced themselves from the rise of Pictorialism, a movement more concerned with personal expression and the creative representation of the feelings and emotions of the photographer. The Survey workers intended to make objective, factual photographic records of their subjects. They wanted nothing that would interfere with the apparent 'truthfulness' of the photograph, so they did not crop or retouch and preferred Platinum printing for its permanence and fine detail. However, their subject matter consisted of a limited antiquarian agenda, where subjects such as notable buildings, 'memorable' events, flora and fauna, meteorology, archeological remains and local institutions such as the church. Routine, mundane events were of little interest as were ordinary people other than as bystanders or representations of unusual or 'colourful' types. Their work was important, however, because it formed the

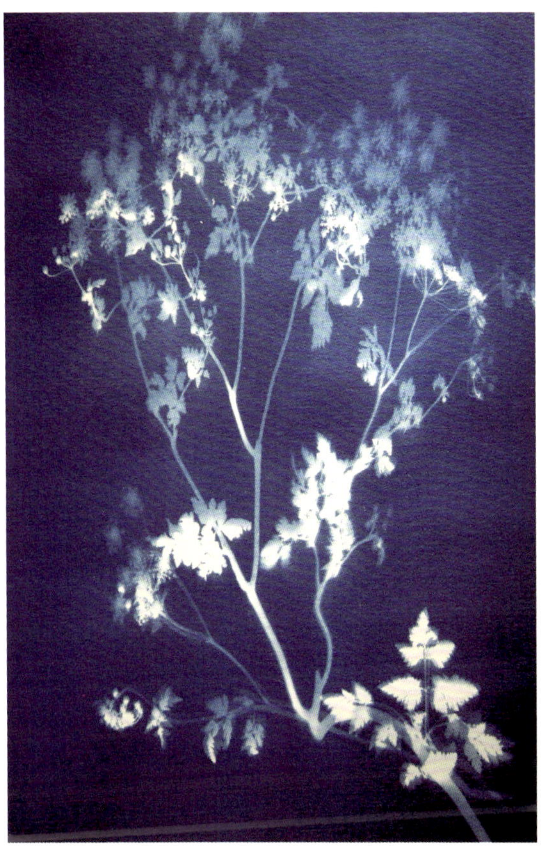

Susan Andrews, *After Anna Atkins, Anthriscus sylvestris (cow parsley)* cyanotype, 2010.

basis of many local history collections and their ideas concerning photographs as historic records have continued to influence thinking in the field.

Recognition of the agenda behind this work led Audrey Linkman to consider some important factors when she came in 1985 to create a new archive, The Contemporary Commissions Collection at The Documentary Photography Archive, Manchester. She acknowledged that "all photographs are produced to an agenda of one kind or another" and that, "photographers working within any given tradition (portraiture, Pictorialism, reportage, etc.) share a set of ideas about the fundamental purpose of their work and adopt common practices and methods of working that enable them to give concrete expression to those abstract ideas. In effect, ideology and methodology work together to shape the generic image."[6] Linkman sees this as a kind of scaffolding which supports the image whilst under construction, so to speak, but is invisible when made. Of course

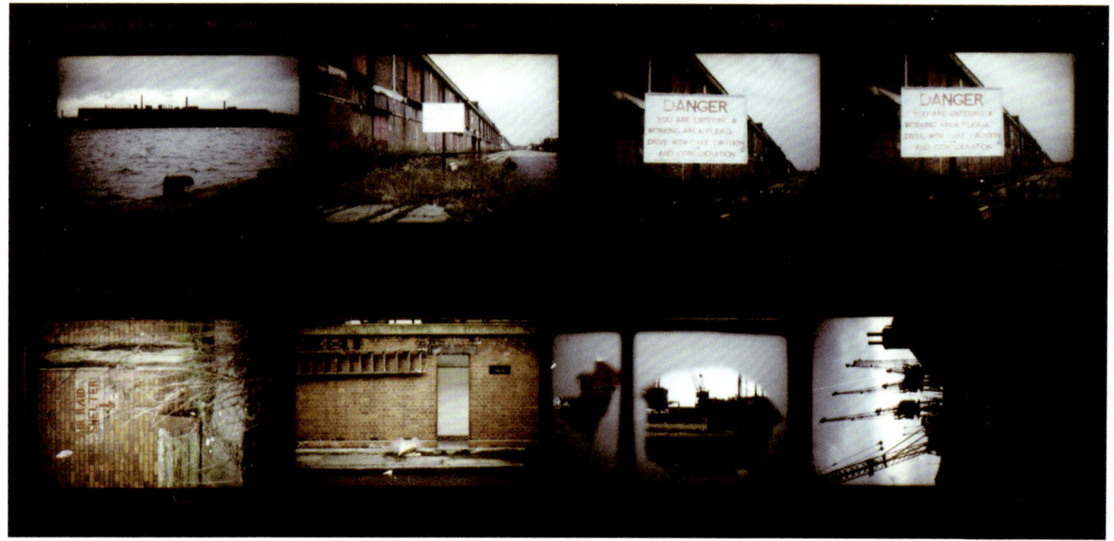

Susan Andrews, Royal Albert Docks (now London City Airport), c. 1980.

ideas and practices will evolve over time and genres will shift, but if historians and photographers are to use images as sources to convey meaning and insight about the past, then it is essential that the framework is understood and is in some way made visible to the researcher.

Linkman chose to address the issue by constructing an archive where she commissioned photographers to produce bodies of work about the ordinary, routine and mundane aspects of everyday life that had mainly gone unrecorded in the past. She also made the very unusual request that, whilst the photographers retained their copyright, all work made for the commission, including negatives, contact sheets, work prints and written information in the form of working diaries and notes were to be deposited in the archive as this "reveals omissions, reflects obsessions... it tells the story of the photographer's journey". Linkman states "to this day I see framed photographs in exhibitions as torn and bleeding around the edges, ripped out of the context that endows them with greater meaning".[7]

Linkman felt that retrospectively, The Contemporary Commissions Collection was more of an experiment in photographic archive making and that some of the commissions had been unsuccessful. However, she hoped that others when making archives in the future would consider the ideas that led to its creation. Certainly, these observations have been influential in setting up the East End Archive at The Cass where we have decided to select only bodies of work from photographers, rather than one off images, along with artists' statements, in order to give the work a context for greater understanding of working methods and subjectivity. This will aid a broad range of researchers in their understanding of the subject and medium. However, whilst Linkman's archives particularly addressed the needs of the historian who uses visual records as sources, The East End Archive, located within The Cass, is also interested in interrogating the collections from a photographic perspective.

Sontag suggests, "each photograph is only a fragment, its moral and emotional weight depends on where it is inserted. A photograph changes according to the context in which it is seen.... As Wittgenstein argued for words, that the meaning is the use—so for each photograph. And it is in this way that the presence and proliferation of all photographs contributes to erosion of the very notion of meaning...".[8] One can certainly acknowledge that photographs do change their meanings based on context but that is not to say that meaning itself is necessarily eroded. Meanings attributed to signs and symbols are all fluid and contingent on an array of aspects including historic perspective and culture. However, by evaluating a body of work rather than a single image, where the many fragments together offer more insight, one may come nearer to understanding the photographer's perspective and original intention.

Nevertheless, in assessing the significance of photographic work within the context of the archive, it is important to recognise that all archivists also work to an agenda that may be personal, institutional or conceptual. One should not overlook the role the archivist plays in constructing meaning, as the design theorist Dhipti Bhagat says, "making the archive becomes performative, constituting as much as documenting the East End".[9] Indeed, archives are mutable places where connotation is dependent on issues such as those selecting the collections, the relationship between the collections themselves and those using the archive. In fact, the reconfiguration of meaning repeats itself each time someone enters the archive, searching for evidence, selecting and editing according to personal interest. As such, the very act of researching becomes another creative act.

Therefore, as a consequence of the many factors that influence our understanding of the photographic work, and key to fully appreciating its potential myriad meanings, it is essential to have insight, precision and transparency. The agenda for building an archive must be clear and the collections organised in such a way as to offer the opportunity to build critical discourse through rigorous engagement with the structures, processes and photographs.

This book is not, of course, the archive itself but functions as a vehicle to discuss issues raised by its construction; consequently, the photography represented in its pages is selected from the broader structure of the digital East End Archive at The Cass. The process of selection inevitably alters our appreciation of the collections, as indeed occurs each time someone engages with a specific aspect of the work. Therefore, interviews with the artists and a series of statements and discussions are reproduced here alongside the photographs, in order to enable debate about the archive itself and explore the significance of photographic practice. It is hoped that these words may offer a starting point for evaluating the construction of meaning by exploring each photographer's journey.

1. Sontag, Susan, "In Plato's Cave", *On Photography*, Harmondsworth: Penguin Books, 1977, p. 5.
2. Moholy-Nagy, Lázló, "From Pigment to Light", *Telehor*, vol. 1, 1936, pp. 32–36.
3. Warner Marien, Mary, *100 Ideas that Changed Photography*, London: Laurence King Publishing, 2012, p. 119.
4. Warner Marien, *100 Ideas that Changed Photography*, p. 119, Underwood and Underwood: stereographic company slogan.
5. Warner Marien, *100 Ideas that Changed Photography*, p. 124.
6. Linkman, Audrey, "Building Archives: Deconstructing Photographs", *Activate 3*, London: Sir John Cass School of Art, 2006, pp. 5–19.
7. Linkman, "Building Archives: Deconstructing Photographs", pp. 5–19.
8. Sontag, Susan, "The Heroism of Vision", *On Photography*, Harmondsworth: Penguin Books, 1977, p. 106
9. Bhagat, Dipti, *Activate 3*, London: Sir John Cass School of Art, 2006, p. 18.

UP AND DOWN WHITECHAPEL HIGH STREET PHOTOGRAPHS FROM THE CAR

SUSAN ANDREWS

The tolerance, the room for great differences among neighbours—differences that often go far deeper than differences in colour... are possible and normal only when streets of great cities have built-in equipment allowing strangers to dwell in peace together on civilised but essentially dignified and reserved terms.

Jane Jacobs, *The Death and Life of Great American Cities*

My daily drive to work takes me past the Bow Interchange to my destination in Aldgate East, travelling along the A11 as it moves towards the City and changes from Bow Road, to Mile End Road, Whitechapel Road and Whitechapel High Street. Historically, this route formed the initial section of the ancient Roman road from London to Colchester but recently it has been known as High Street 2012, which connects the City to the Olympic Park. This route runs through some of the most disadvantaged neighbourhoods in London, but it also moves through historically rich areas and some of the most culturally diverse. During the build up to the Olympic games it was the site of increased development and activity.

In late 2008, I decided to alleviate the frustration of the heavy traffic caused by road works, incidents and accidents, by taking a photograph each time the traffic stopped. I set myself a system where I only photograph when the car is stationary with the handbrake on, which means there are no snatched images, but there are no rules regarding the direction of the shot or the subject matter, just whatever takes my eye. These photographs have a particular aesthetic as the vantage point is from the car, where passers-by are often viewed side-on in relation to buildings which face the camera, offering a very different perspective than from the pavement.

Over time, a document of the ever-shifting life of the road has been built up based both on arbitrary stops and starts of the traffic, and patterns to its flow relating to current street activity. The project marks changes: changes in space, season, time, and direction as I make my return journey home.

In *The View from the Road*, Donald Appleyard suggests that "the modern car interposes a filter between the driver and the world he is moving through. Sounds, smells, sensations of touch and weather are all diluted in comparison with what the pedestrian experiences."[1] Surprisingly then, one of the interesting aspects of this project has been that, despite the filter of the car, photography has enabled me to reconnect with my surroundings. The camera has facilitated a sense of individual relationship with the immediate environment rather than functioning, as

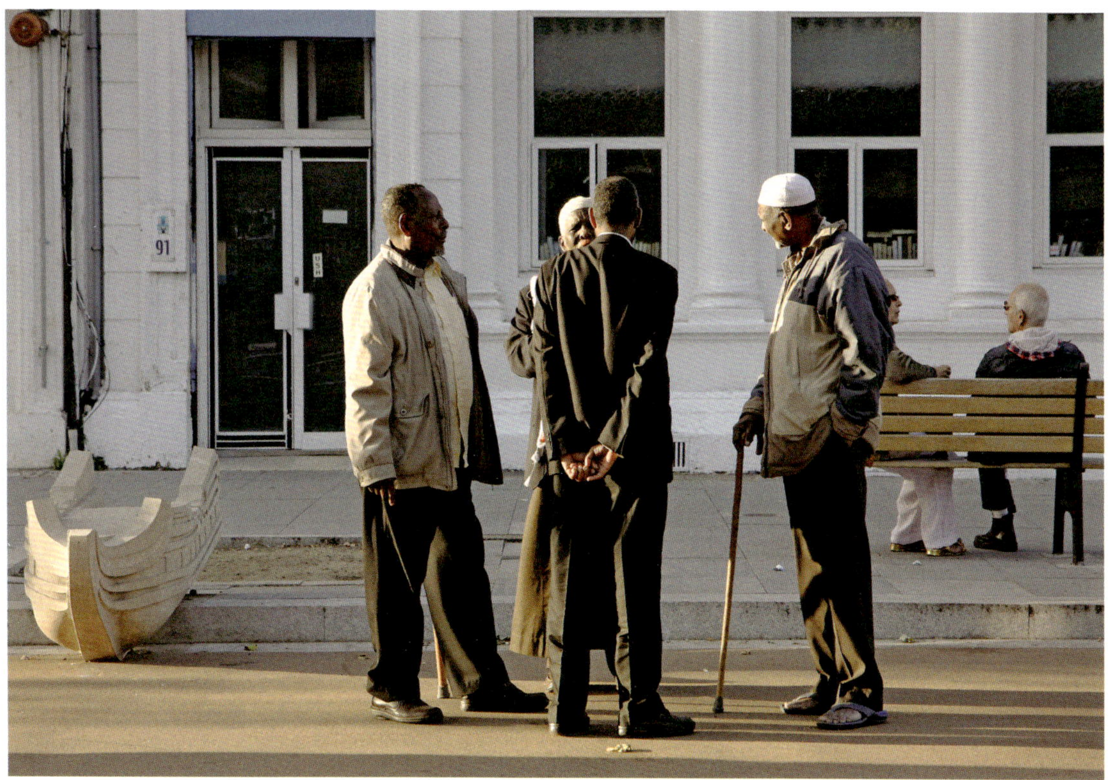

Susan Andrews, from the series *Up and Down Whitechapel High Street,* A11, 2012.

Sontag comments, as "a powerful instrument for depersonalising our relation to the world".[2] I no longer dread the erratic nature of the journey to work but look forward to recording the ongoing architectural transformations and capricious street life, enjoying the constant flux (an extraordinary amount in these few years) and the immensely diverse population that the road offers.

In the 1960s the urban philosopher Jane Jacobs had been critical of the modernist planners of the period who rejected the multi-layered, complex and apparently chaotic nature of the city, preferring rather to segregate aspects of living e.g., residential, industrial and commercial. She felt that such policies were destructive, and advocated density, high pedestrian permeability, buildings of various ages in different states of repair and mixed use of the streets.[3] Looking at the Whitechapel High Street today, one is struck by how much it appears to embody her vision of a functioning and diverse city community.

1. Appleyard, Donald, Kevin Lynch and John R Myer, *View from the Road*, Cambridge, MA: MIT Press, 1964, p. 106.
2. Sontag, Susan, *On Photography*, Harmondsworth: Penguin Books, 1977, p. 167.
3. Jacobs, Jane, *The Death and Life of Great American Cities*, New York: Random House, 1961.

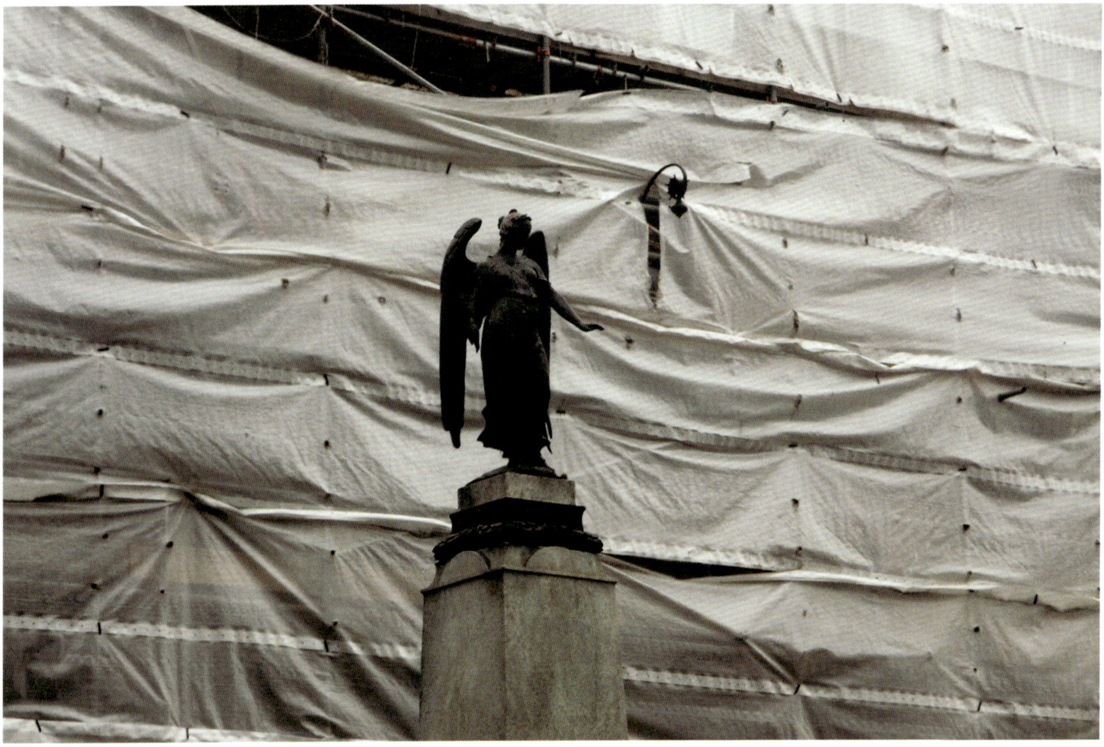

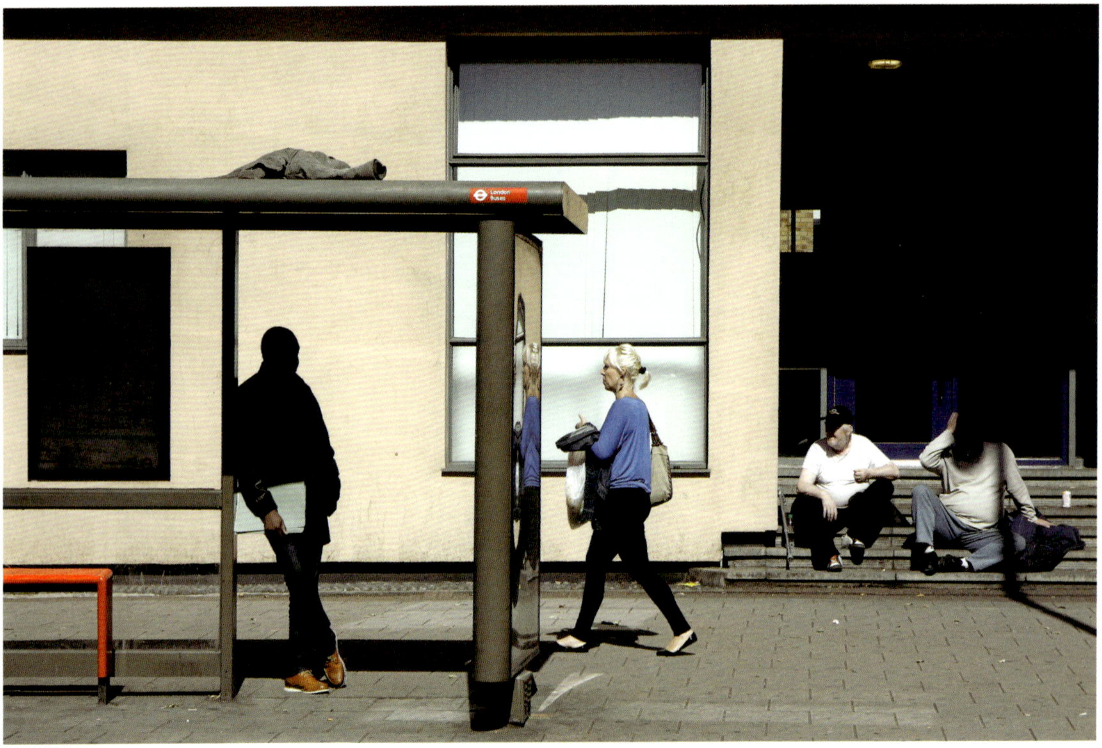

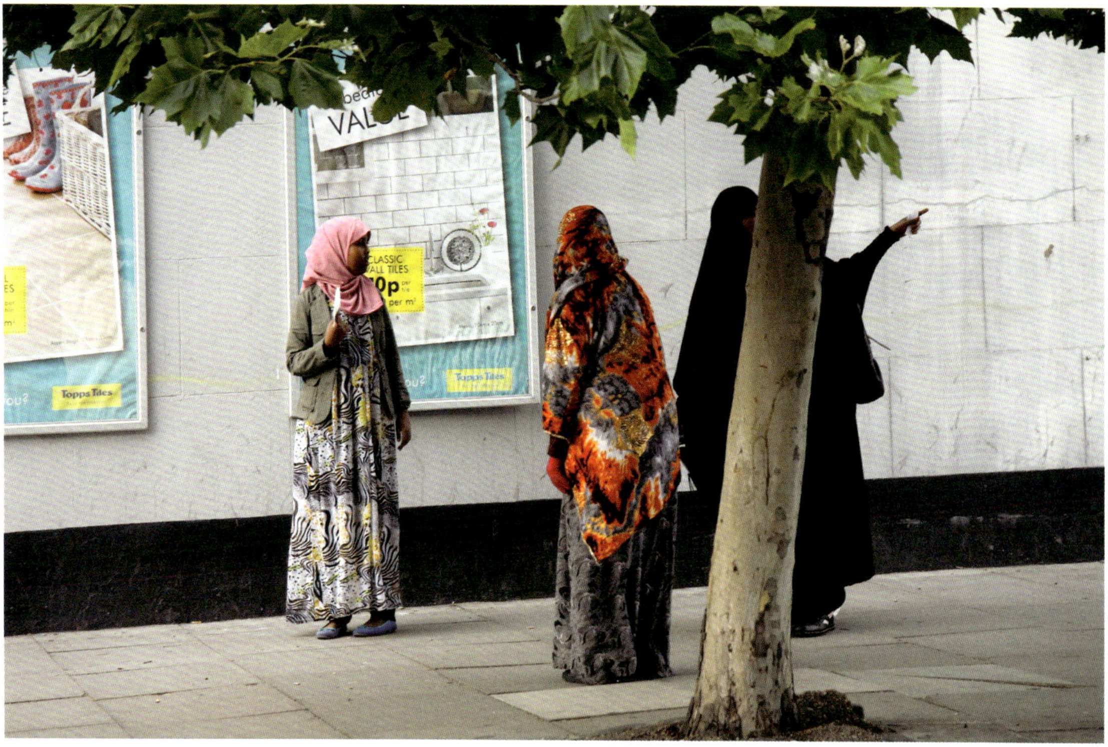

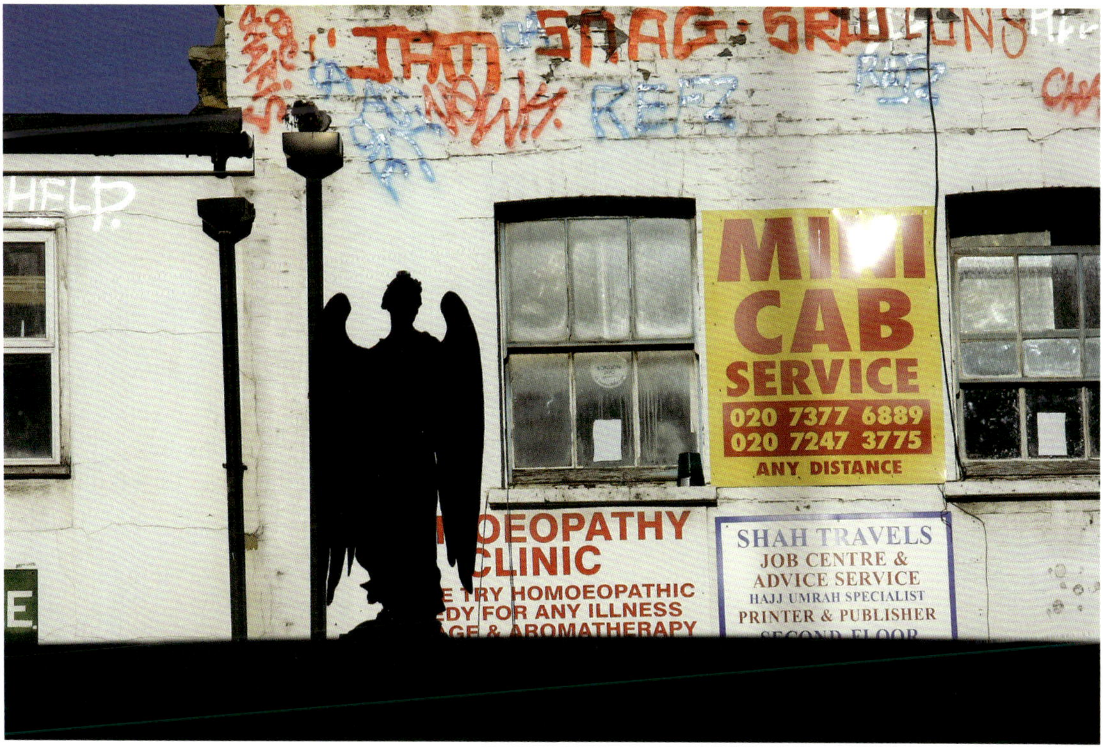

Susan Andrews, from the series *Up and Down Whitechapel High Street*, A11, clockwise from opposite top: 2013, 2012, 2009, 2012.
Overleaf: Susan Andrews, from the series *Up and Down Whitechapel High Street*, A11, 2010.

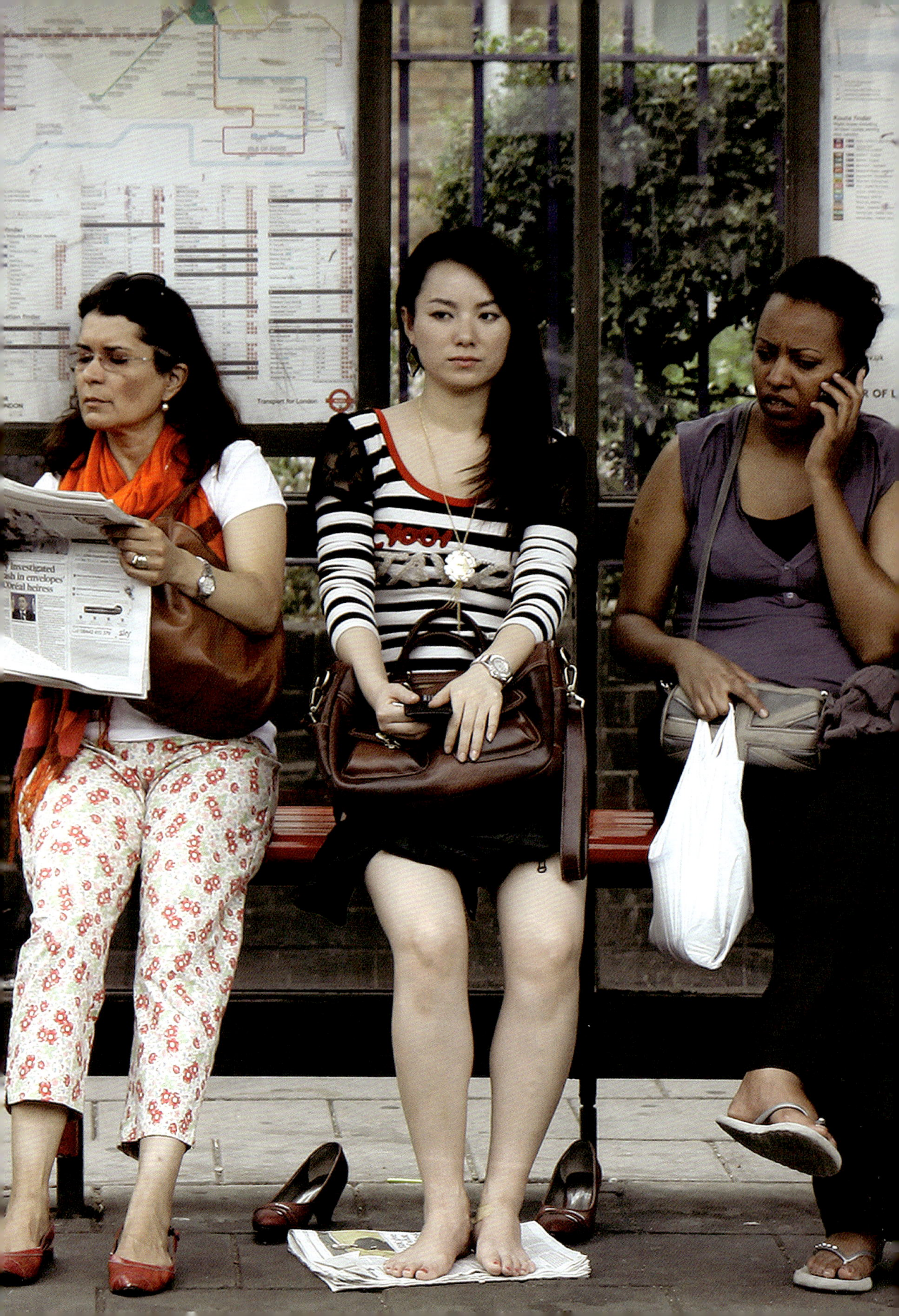
Investigated

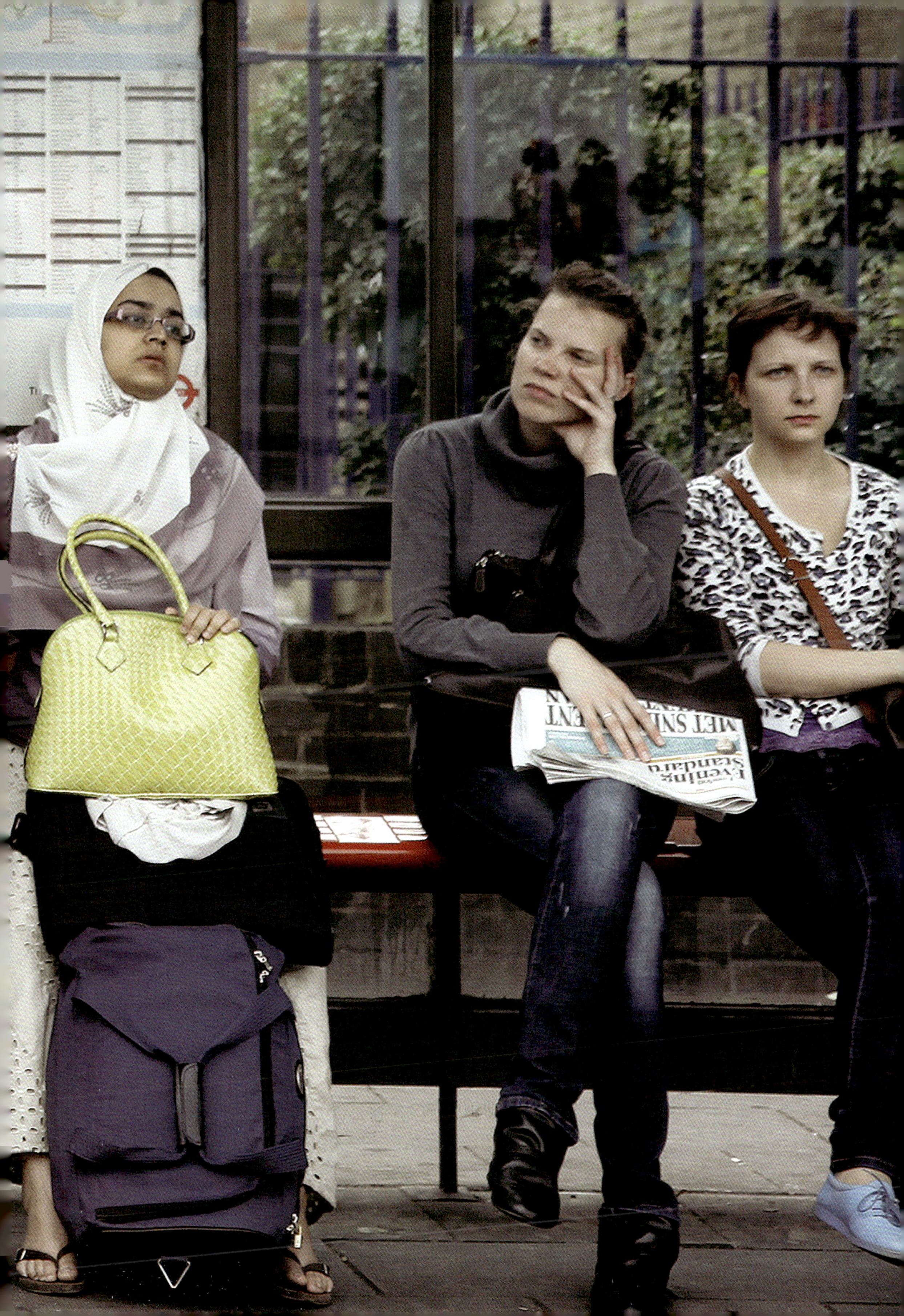
Evening Standard

PANORAMA HIGH STREET EAST 2012

THE BUILDING EXPLORATORY

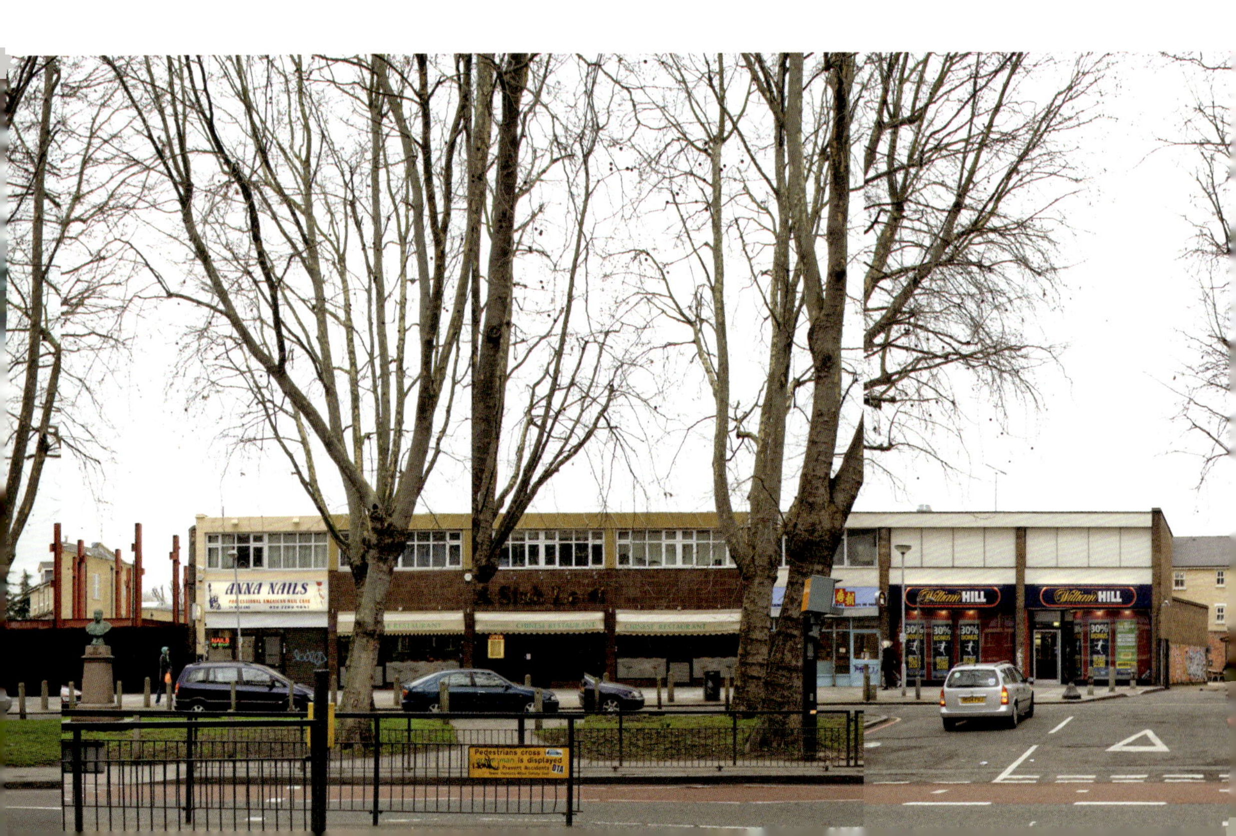

At the very start of this project I took a bus ride, first from Aldgate to Bow Church and then back again. The journey revealed the great variations in scale, style and period of the buildings along this road and also how the street slips from one character to another in different areas.

Looking at the finished result, one of the things I find very striking is the sense of the road as a canyon—with the roofline being this very dramatic and dynamic thing that bounces around, up and down, describing all of these different shapes, modern canopies to Georgian chimney pots, Victorian decoration to an innocuous post-war box.

A ride on the 205 to Bow Church is never going to be the same again.

Jon Spencer

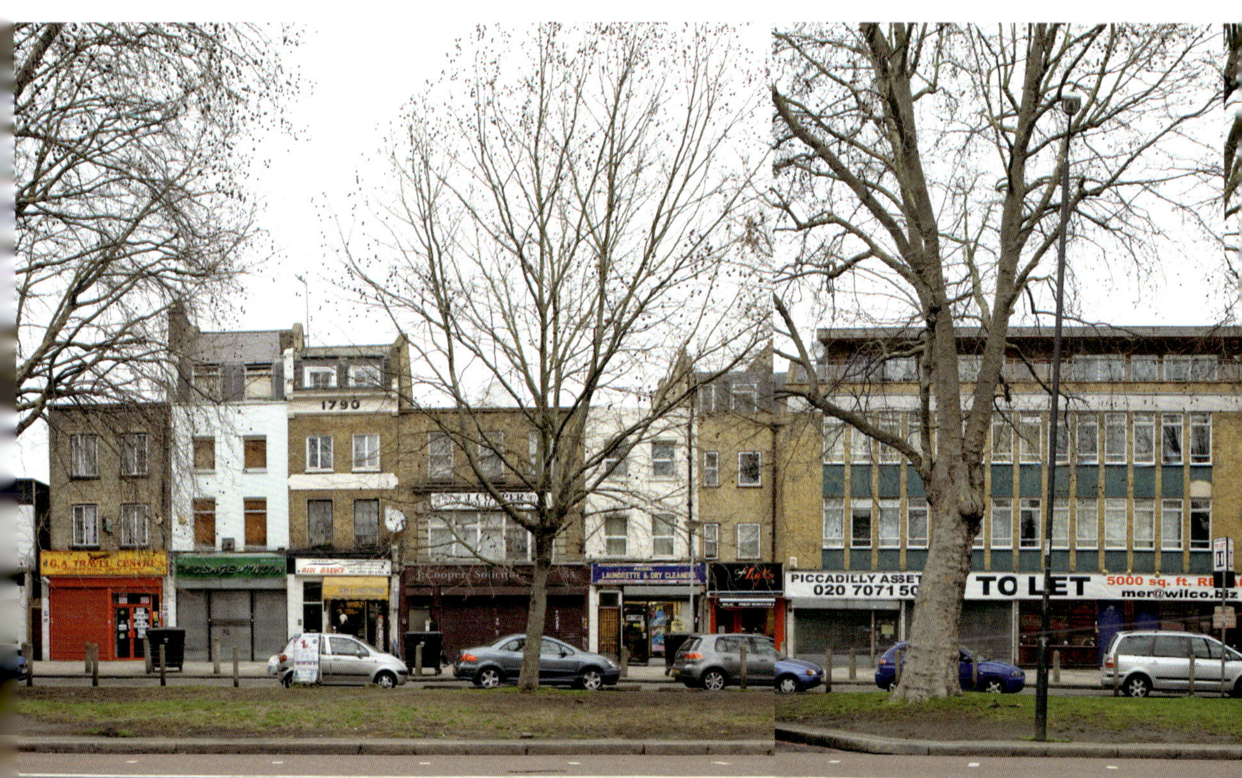

69–89 Mile End Road
Wickham's

Completed: 1927
Built by: Thomas Jay Evans
Historic period: Inter-war: 1919–1939
This is a significant building
Current Use: Retail

The Wickham family were originally drapers, trading from 69, 71 and 73 Mile End Road. No. 75 was occupied by the Spiegelhalter family business of clockmakers and jewellers. With the Wickhams' continuing success, in about 1892 they agreed with the Spiegelhalters that they (the Spiegelhalters) would move a few doors up the road from 75 to 81 Mile End Road so that the Wickhams could take over and expand into the shop at no. 75.

35 years later the Wickham family had acquired the entire block except the Spiegelhalter's shop at no. 81 and had planned a major rebuilding of their shop. This time the Spiegelhalter family refused to part with their premises at any price. Their refusal to move led to the odd situation in which the new store was built around the family shop which continued to trade when Wickham's opened on both its sides.

The Building Exploratory, *Panorama High Street East 2012*, Whitechapel High Street, 2012.

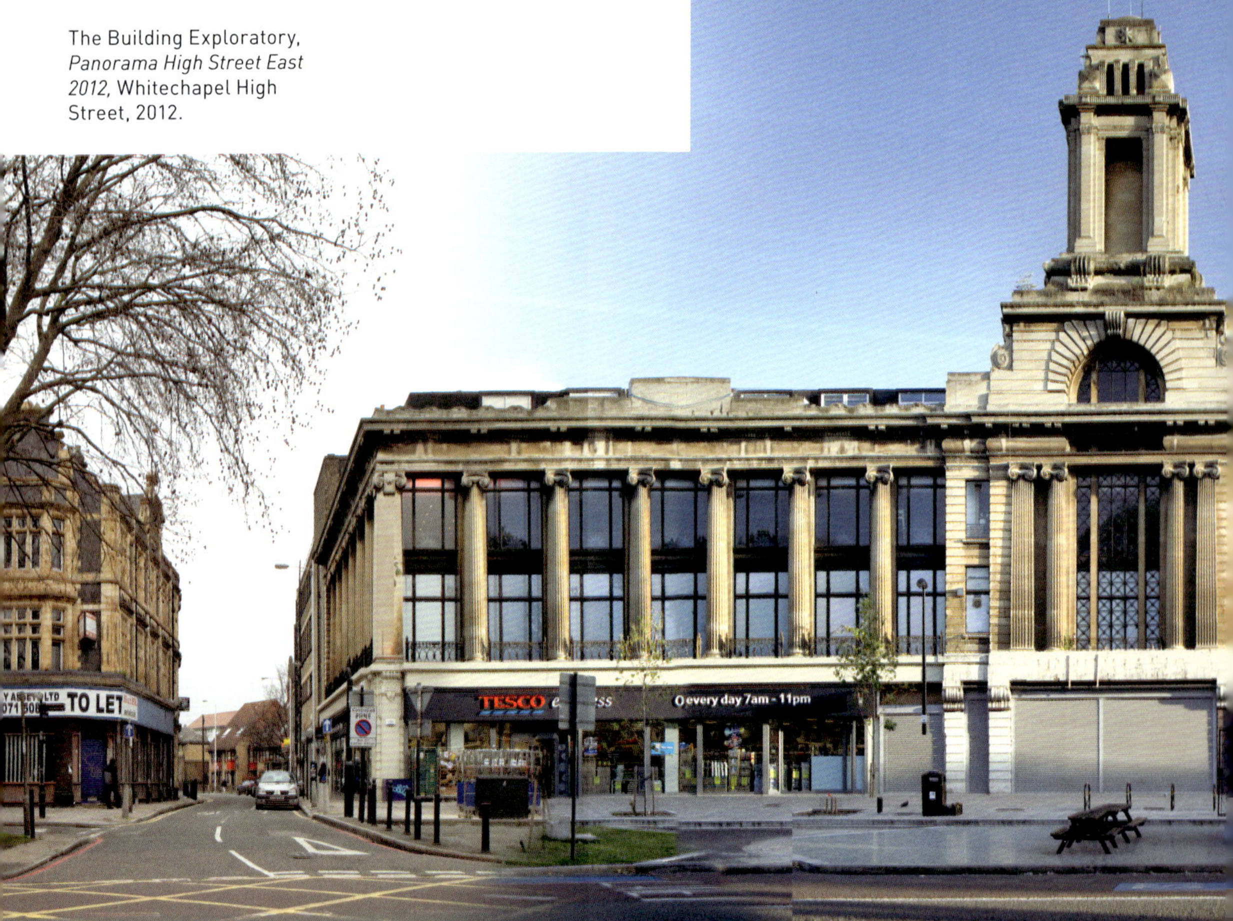

93–95 Mile End Road
Genesis Cinema

Completed: 1939
Built by: W R Glen
Historic period: Inter-war: 1919–1939
This is a significant building
Current Use: Entertainment

This building has been providing entertainment services for over 150 years. From the Eagle Public House, 1848, Lusby's Music Hall, Paragon Theatre of Varieties, 1885, Mile End Empire, 1912, ABC Mile End, 1960, to finally the Genesis Cinema. During the time the cinema was the Paragon Music Hall, Charlie Chaplin performed here before he was famous.

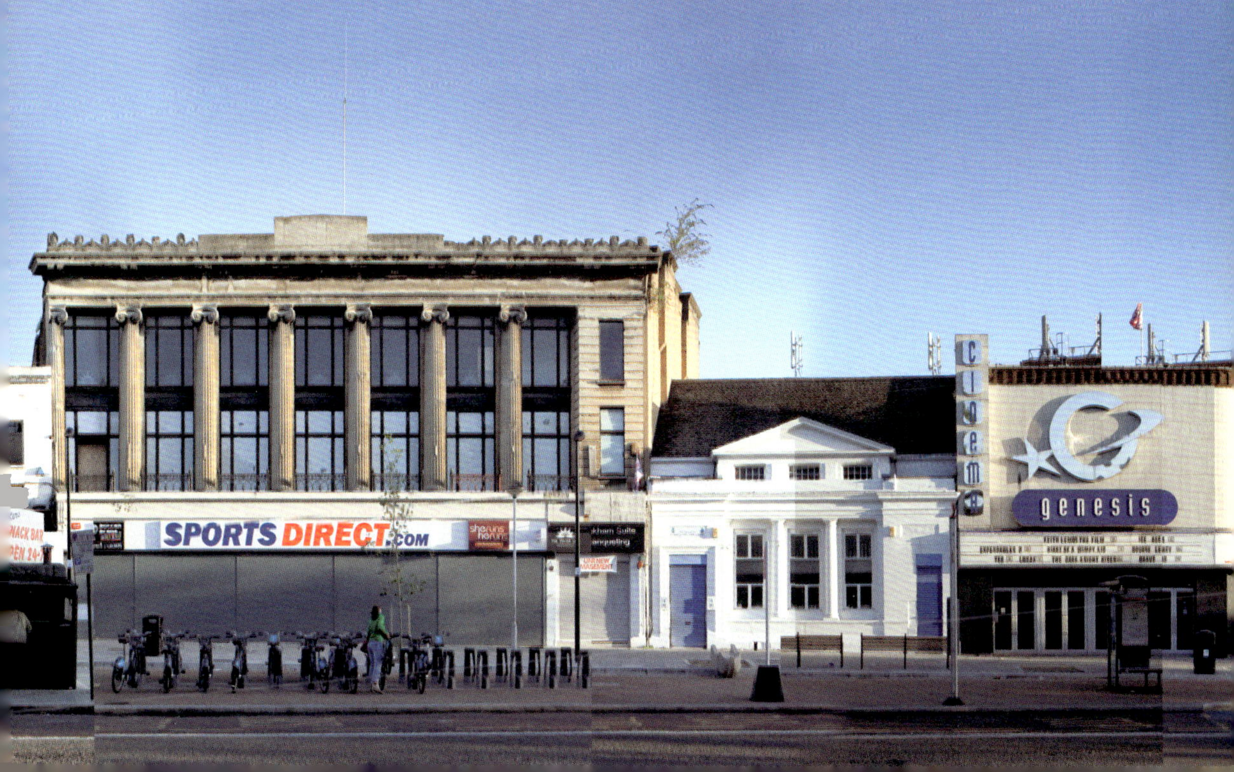

THE PARALYMPIANS

IAN FARRANT IN CONVERSATION WITH MICHAEL UPTON

MICHAEL UPTON The *Paralympians* series was part of your work for the MA course at The Cass?

IAN FARRANT Yes

MU When did the photography take place—was the intention to look at the London 2012 Olympics?

IF In early 2011 and yes, that was completely the plan. I knew they were happening, I knew that as a former wheelchair rugby player I had connections I could follow up and access to the athletes, and of course I was studying in the East End so it made sense

MU What drew you to the project?

IF I played wheelchair rugby, so I had an interest in how athletes are photographed. As far as I could see no disabled photographer had taken images of our Paralympians, which seemed strange. The images out there were sports action shots or pedestrian-looking, run-of-the-mill press shots, passport photographs even. I wanted to look at the Paralympians in a different way.

I was interested in how, as a disabled person, with a wheelchair level view, I would take these images in terms of how the photographs would look from that level and of the rapport I might have with the subjects as a fellow disabled athlete, and how that might come through in the work. The subjects were really responsive and supportive,

Opposite: Ian Farrant, *Ian Day, wheelchair fencing*, 2011.

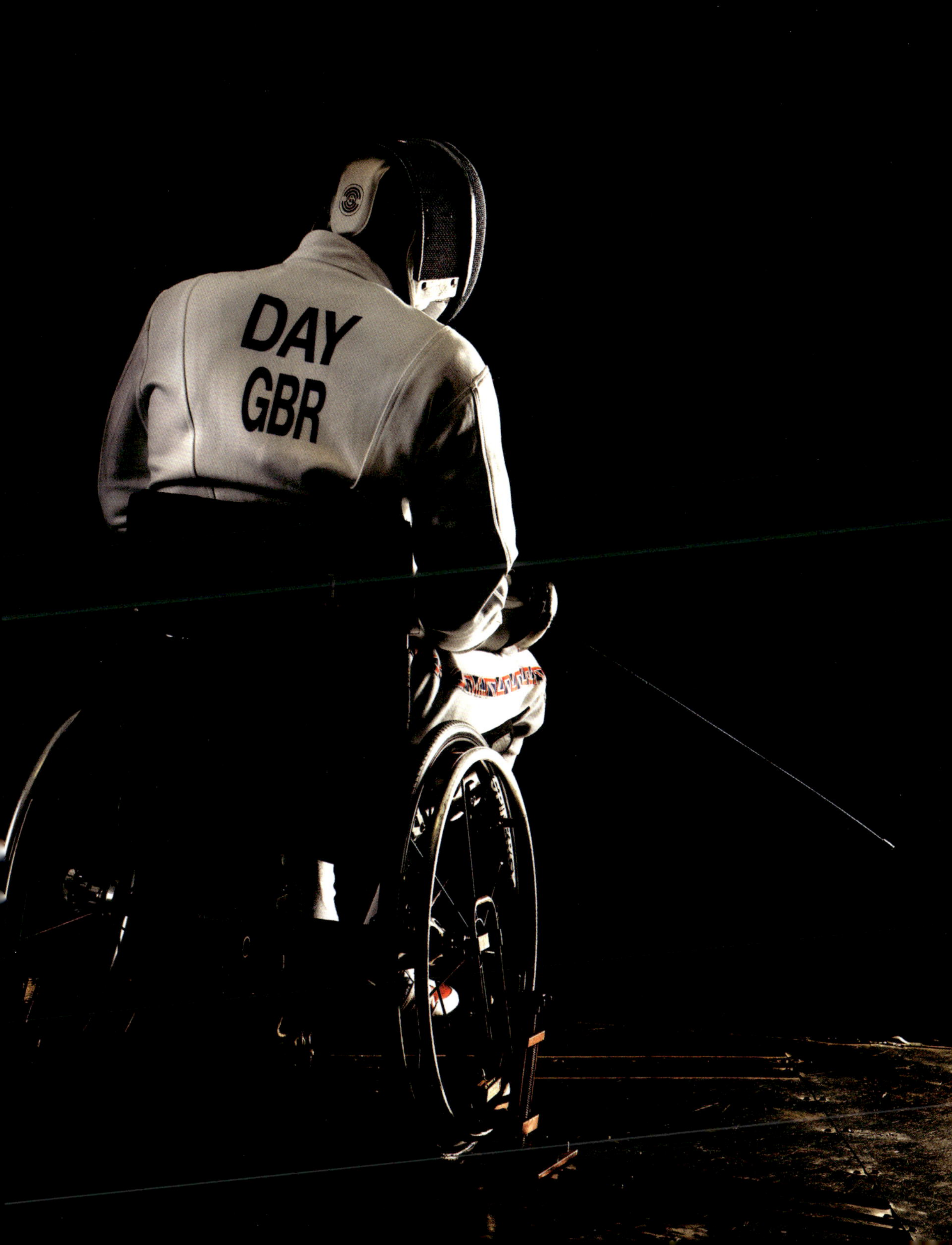
DAY
GBR

taking time out for me, connecting well. Shots of Paralympians had often been taken by standing photographers—I was 'on a level' in more ways than one.

MU You shot on location but there seems to be a very deliberate controlled environment.

IF It was always a studio set up, on location—the athletes were in their familiar space but it was equally very staged. I wanted them to be in a 'set' and not distracted by anyone or anything else. From my perspective I wanted the control of the shot, and for the viewer to look at the person or the action—again without any distraction.

MU How did these differ from previous images of Paralympians?

IF I think that the portraits are very warm, that as well as the physical connection there was a psychological one, and because I'd been a player there was that connection too. I also think that there is a group of severely disabled people who were and remain invisible despite all the 'coverage' of the Paralympians during the games. They travel the world, representing their country, they are European and world champions—but invisible ones.

MU There seem to be two types of shot, you could say 'nouns' and 'verbs', portraits of people and shots of people in action. And within that there may even be a third—some of the portraits could be described as epic/heroic.

IF I knew I wasn't going to get another chance like this. So I planned to take different types of image within the time constraints. The portraits were designed to make a connection with the person. They are looking into the lens, so the viewer's gaze is directed to look at the person in the shot. In the other photographs I intended to capture the feeling of strenuous effort or the physicality of the sports. In the fencing series with the seated man shot from the back, the intention was to show him bowing his head, wilting after furious exertion, to say, "this is a man who's put everything into it".

MU Was there a conscious political or social agenda?

IF I didn't start out with something 'political' to say as such, with a message but that idea of invisibility and of seeing a certain group from a specific vantage.

MU Some of the images anticipate the 'superhuman' theme that emerged in the Paralympics coverage—what did you think about the representation of Paralympians/Paralympic sports in the games?

IF I liked the advert Channel Four ran. During that campaign all eyes were on the disabled. But to me, well, it got chucked on Channel Four, not the BBC, marginalised to a certain extent. And any mainstream coverage it got was limited—it always focused on obvious cover stars.

MU I sensed some similarities between your 'veteran' and 'Paralympian' projects—the notion of representation of the individual versus 'hero'.

IF This was about seeing the people beyond the disability and beyond context—much like seeing the individual Chelsea Pensioners beyond the red uniforms. I didn't want to get the 'sympathy vote' from the audience but rather for them to look and respond to the images.

MU How important is the East End archive project?

IF It's very important. This is a rich and changing part of London. Over the years Jews, Bangladeshi, French have come here and well it's got a sense of being a starting place for everyone. These images in the archive are a record of different aspects of that journey.

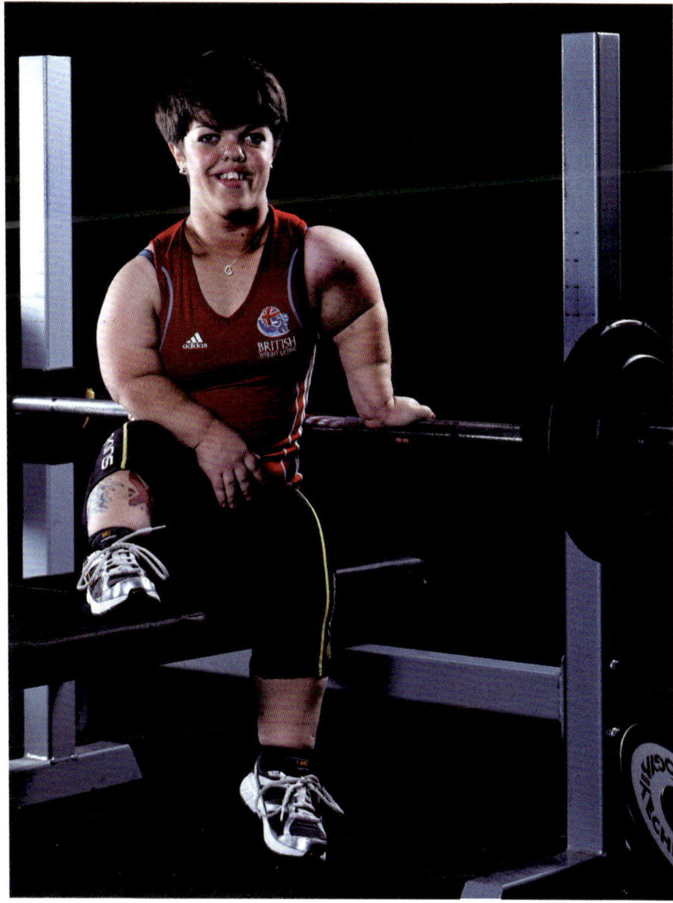

Ian Farrant, *Roxan Luckock, 48kg power-lifter,* 2011.

SITES OF AFRICA

JOY GREGORY, WORDS BY ROHINI MALIK OKON

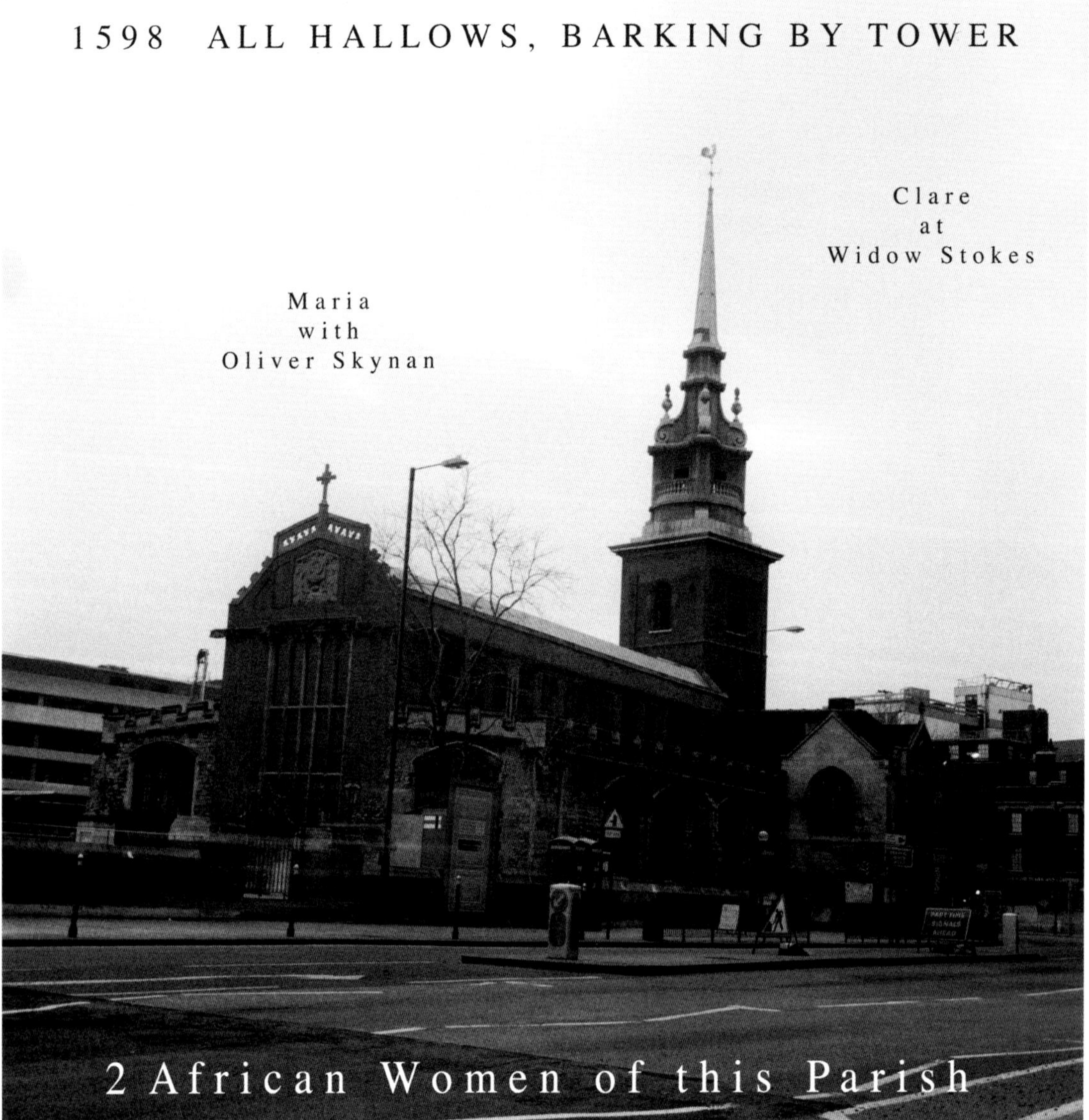

Joy Gregory, *All Hallows*, from the series *Sites of Africa*, 2010.
Overleaf: Joy Gregory, *Bank of England*, from the series *Sites of Africa*, 2010.

In her photographic series *Sites of Africa*, Joy Gregory brings to the city's surface an array of untold histories, both individual and collective, as she reinscribes into the urban lexicon the insistent whispers of narratives, forgotten, unheard and long buried. Each of the London locations represented in these images was once associated with an African presence, yet through time any traces alluding to that presence have been erased and the sites are now associated with more recent events. Quietly insistent and with a sense of emptiness and stillness, Gregory's photographic works appear to be both documenting an absence and asserting a presence as they seek to address the invisibility of these histories in contemporary public space.

These eight works, focused specifically on the City of London, are part of a larger series exposing the history of a black presence in the metropolis over the past few hundred years. With their close proximity to the familiar everyday splendour of Canary Wharf and Docklands, the sites and the stories that Gregory has chosen to reveal invite us to reflect upon the largely unacknowledged source of much of the City of London's wealth. We are reminded that the rapid growth of the City's commercial and material infrastructure in the seventeenth and eighteenth centuries was rooted in the transatlantic slave trade, and that the river and the docks are also part of this narrative. City of London investors and institutions both funded and profited from the slave trade, providing credit and insurance for slaving voyages and reaping substantial financial rewards from the cargoes of sugar, tobacco and cotton that arrived in London's docks from the Caribbean.

Established in 1694, the Bank of England was set up to create a viable financial system for England's expanding transatlantic economy, and was thus instrumental in funding plantation slavery and the slave trade. As one of Gregory's *Sites of Africa*, the story she unearths here suggests another association and reveals a moment of dissent and empowerment rather than enslavement. The Bank of England was one of the institutions attacked during the Gordon Riots at a time of civil unrest in the late-eighteenth century, and black rioters were among the mob. Previously untold narratives of resistance haunt a number of the images in this series, e.g. the serenity of Gregory's *Tower Hill* belies this site's turbulent past as a place of execution and the individual tale here told of an eighteenth century black woman's defiance, while Brick Lane adds a further layer to our knowledge of this site as a locus historically both for migration and for protest.

Another site, Mincing Lane, has a multilayered connection with both the slave trade and its abolition, which the artist alludes to in the story she relays of Granville Sharp and Jonathan Strong. This street was home to prominent slave traders including the founder of Barings Bank, which was set up to finance slave trading voyages, as well as to the lawyer Granville Sharp who was one of the earliest campaigners for the rights of black people in Britain.

Alerting us to the fact that physical sites hold memory and that places bear witness—both to monumental events and to individual experiences—Gregory, in this eloquent photographic series, takes on the role of both excavator and storyteller. The tales that resurface in these works evoke a multiplicity of black histories once present within the City of London, and not those solely associated with the slave trade. The stark, bleak stillness of *Down River to Ratcliff* is at odds with the cited 'influx', yet makes all the more poignant the plight of these soldiers, their collective endeavour washed away by the Thames. Addressing the commonly held, but mistaken, perception that London's black population is a relatively recent phenomenon, *Sites of Africa* asserts that there has been black presence in London for hundreds of years. The viewer is invited to consider e.g. who were the two African women of the Parish of All Hallows and how did they come to live in London at the end of the sixteenth century?

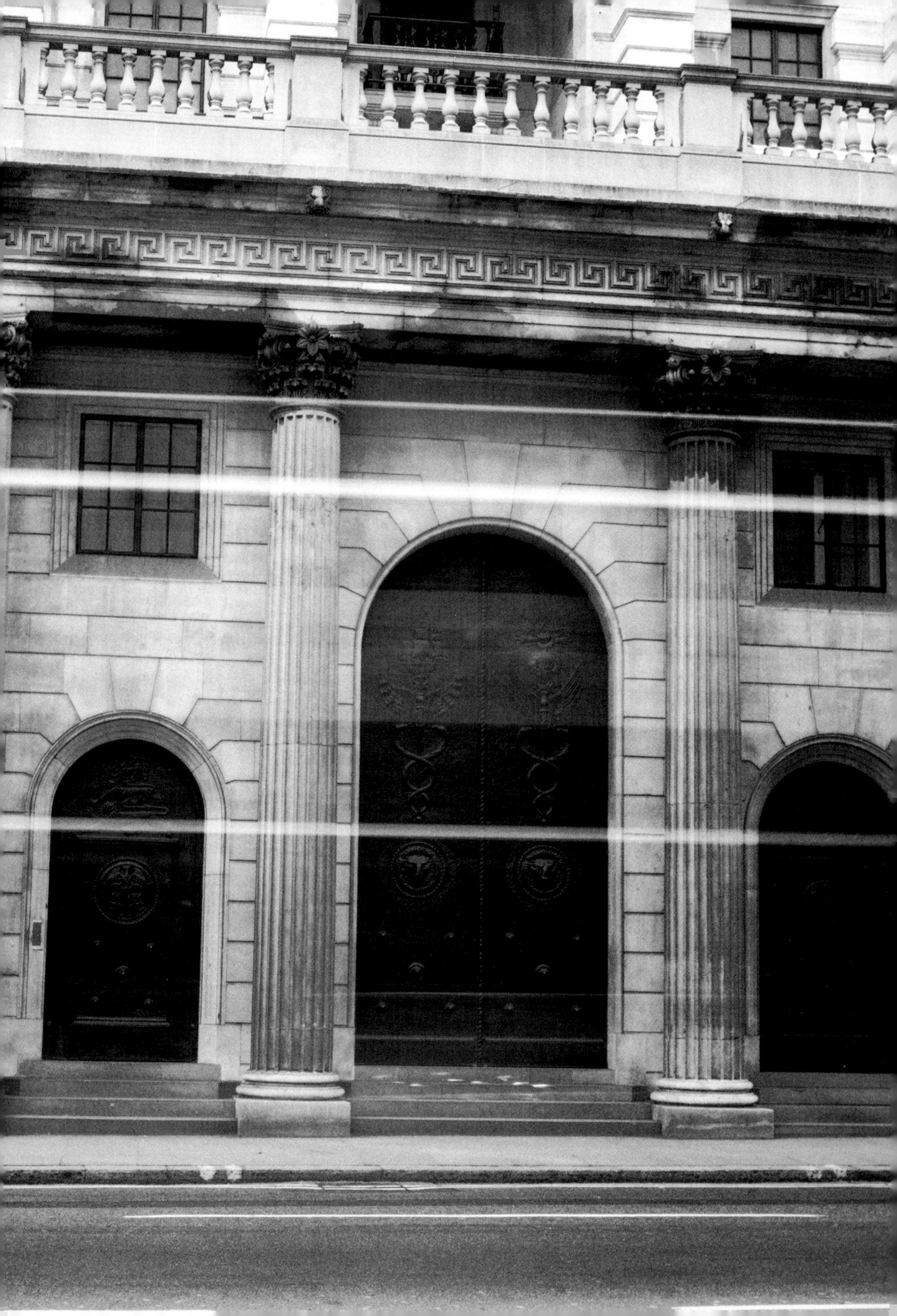

1778

Attacked by 'Mob' during the Gordon Riots

BANK OF ENGLAND

Illustrations of the day show members of the black population took an active part

THE BROADGATE PROJECT

BRIAN GRIFFIN
WORDS BY SUSAN ANDREWS

The work of Brian Griffin in the 1980s was in many ways in keeping with the staged documentary practice that started to evolve at the time with artists such as Jeff Wall. Griffin constructed narratives in collaboration with those portrayed to investigate relationships between subject, photographer and commissioner. Griffin utilised playful references to art history, contemporary symbols and visual puns in order to construct a complex document that formed a commentary on the era. His practice represents both a subjective and inventive process, which he was able to explore despite the fact that much of the work was initially made for corporate organisations. However, unlike many photographers, he saw no distinction between personal artwork and his commercial output, stating, "I was essentially a commercial photographer, even though my commercial work would always go on gallery walls... I would turn my commercial work into my own work, by taking it personally."[1]

In many ways Griffin's photographic approach was exemplified in his commission for the development company Rosehaugh Stanhope to document the City of London's *Broadgate Project*, which was under construction between 1985–1990. Broadgate is an office and retail estate that covers 32 acres and is located on the original site of Broad Street station and beside the railway approaches to Liverpool Street Station. Originally, part of the site had been situated

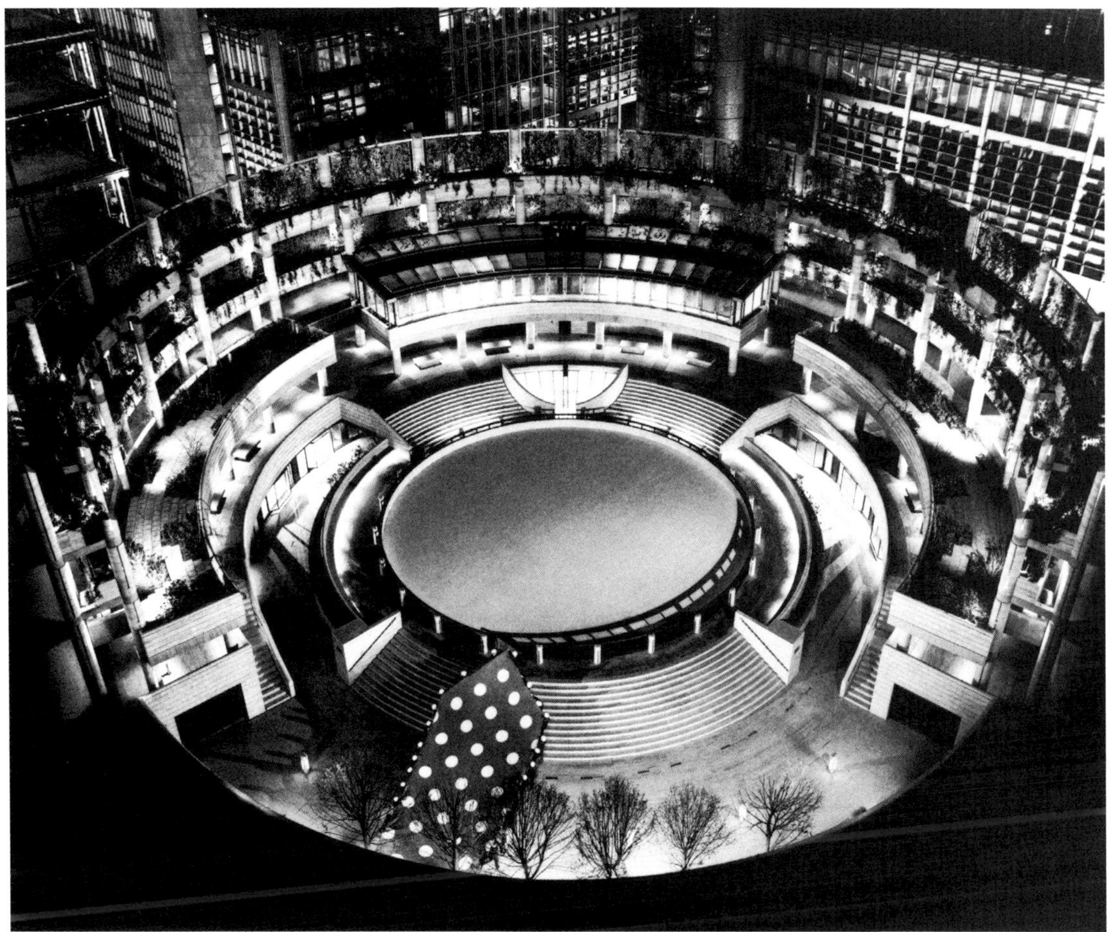

Brian Griffin, *Big Tie*, from the *Broadgate Project*, 1987.

in the London Borough of Hackney but boundary changes made in 1994 now place the entire estate within the City of London. These shifting boundaries reflect changes to the traditionally defined borders of the East End, as areas have been developed and gentrified so that the East End moves ever outwards.

The Broadgate development was built in a period of boom in both the financial and property markets and it pioneered new methods of fast construction. Griffin's photographic approach reflected the innovative techniques; he was interested in exploring new possibilities, pushing the medium both technically and aesthetically and this project in many ways represented the epitome of his exploration of new methods of documenting and photographing what was normally seen as mundane subject matter.

Griffin's work often developed through quick-thinking responses to situations that presented themselves. One afternoon in 1987 whilst an executive was showing a model of the new development to some clients his tie swung into the model; the tie was an 80s emblem of young upwardly mobile professionals (yuppies) and Griffin recognised this as an opportunity to explore the symbolism further. Consequently, he conceived *The Big Tie* series of photographs for the corporate promotional publication and ended it with *Big Bang*, a photographed explosion in the middle of the building construction site that refers to the

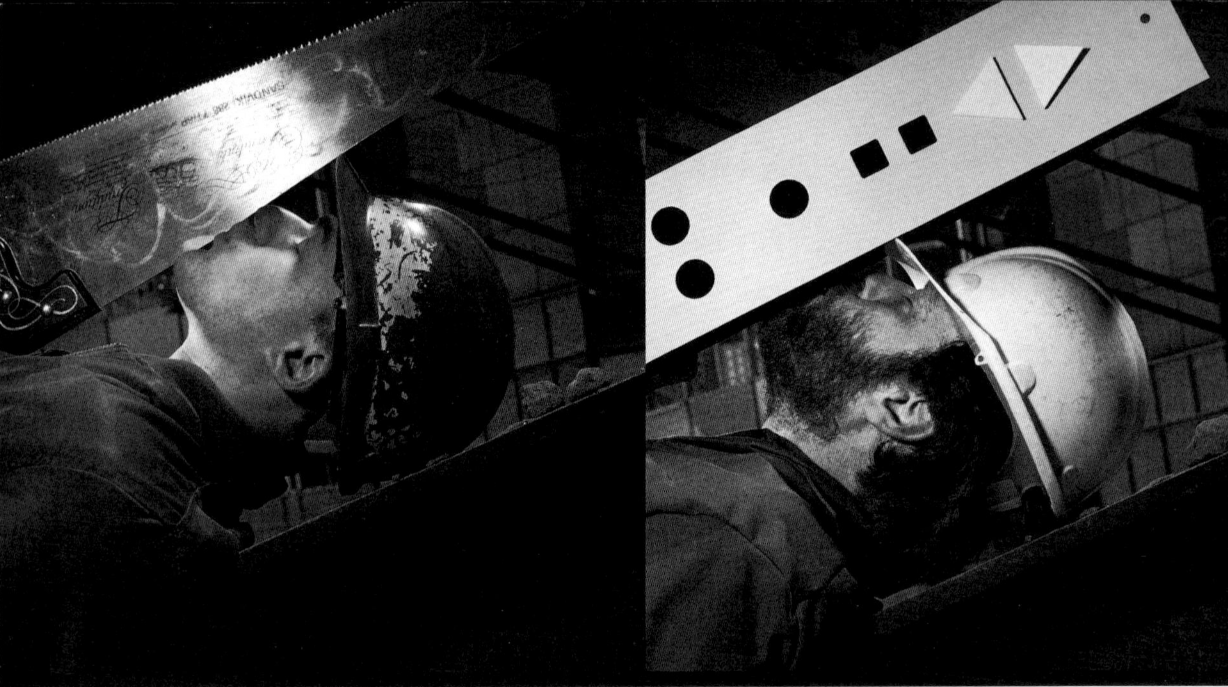

Brian Griffin, *Carpenter, Lift Engineer, Plasterer, Sewage Pipe Layer*, from the *Broadgate Project*, 1986.

deregulation of the financial markets in 1986. This documentation of the development was constructed in a manner reminiscent of film sets where large-scale lighting, giant model ties and numerous participants were utilised to create a vision of a brave new future.

However, when Griffin was asked by the company to photograph a Broadgate subject of his own choice, he turned his attention to a different group of City workers. At the time he was still mourning the loss of his father who died from industrial pollution, so he chose to photograph the construction workers, builders and artisans, many of whom he represented as effigies of knights lying on their tombs. Some images of the workers are also reminiscent of Constructivist imagery where the subjects assume heroic status. This reverential work was both a eulogy to his father and a tribute to all the manual tradesmen who were so often overlooked.

Griffin had the ability to clearly understand the times in which he operated and to mirror this in his work. He suggested alternative ways of interpreting the era through approaching his photography with great skill and invention. Indeed, this work may reveal a great deal more about the times than traditional 'straight' documentary photography as it engages with visually representing the aspirations and attitudes of the time. He recognised that the photographer can construct

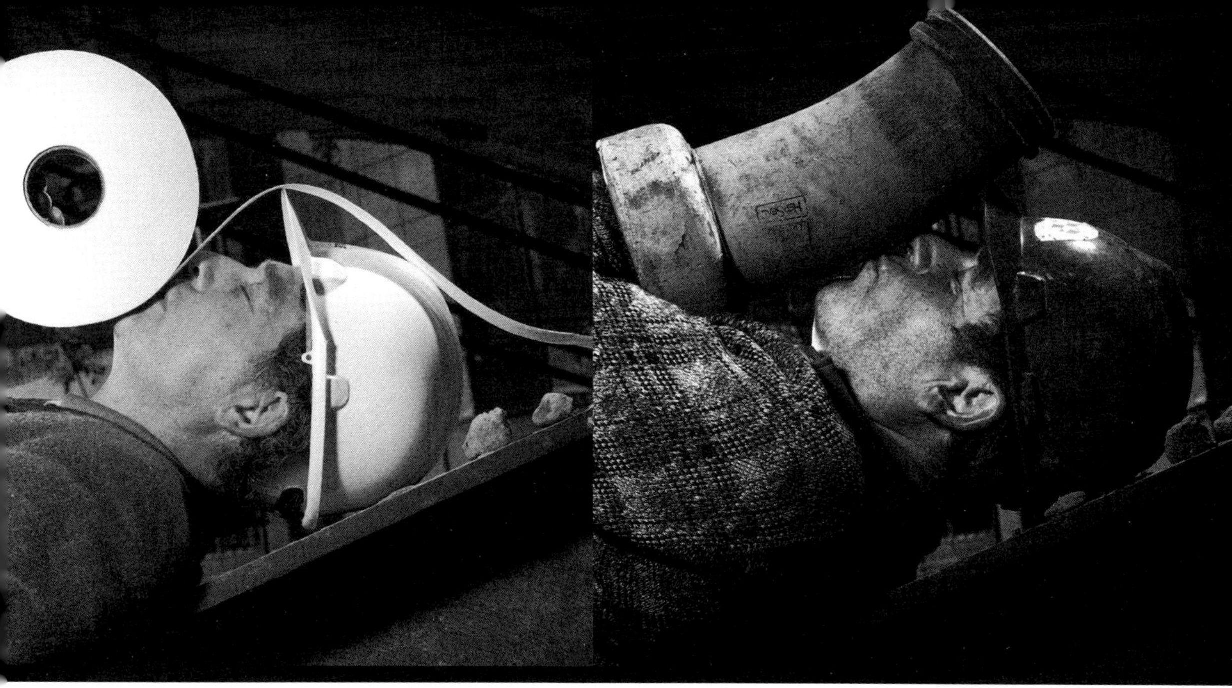

a narrative by editing together various parts of the story, in much the same way as a journalist or filmmaker and still retain integrity in story-telling. In fact, the transparency of the constructed image may allow for the viewer to engage more easily with the issues it raises, rather than indulging in anxiety over whether a 'straight' image is indeed authentic. Johanna Drucker has written about the crisis of traditional documentary photography in an image-saturated culture, and the subsequent loss of faith in the ability of photographs to witness reliably. Drucker proposes a new term, "refamiliarisation" where she argues that it is time for art to reveal the forces behind its making and reconnect with lived experience.[2]

1. Interview with the photographer, 13 May 2012.

2. Drucker, Johanna, "Making Space: Image Events in an Extreme State", in Francis Frascina, ed., *Modern Art Culture: A Reader*, London and New York: Routledge, 2008, pp. 25–45.

SHADOWS OF DOUBT

NICHOLAS HAEFFNER

In 2011, I was approached by David George, a former student on the MA in Photography at London Metropolitan University, who showed me some images he had taken at night in Leytonstone. David had started to think about the somewhat gothic atmosphere of his images in connection with Alfred Hitchcock's childhood, some of which was spent in Leytonstone. He reasoned that Hitchcock would have passed through many of the areas photographed and began to wonder whether some of the strange and gloomy surroundings could have had some influence on Hitchcock's later aesthetic. I shared a few colourful anecdotes about Hitchcock's childhood which led us to invite one of David's frequent collaborators, Spencer Rowell (another student on the MA Photography), to contribute some of his ongoing work on representing childhood trauma through photography for an exhibition on the theme of Hitchcock's East End childhood.

We were keen to emphasise the unreliable nature of Hitchcock's own recollections about his childhood so the images in the project were designed to exploit the doubt and uncertainty about Hitchcock's early life. Many people, most influentially, perhaps his biographer Donald Spoto, see the origin of Hitchcock's work in his childhood, but what do we really know about his childhood experiences? Was he, as he often claimed, actually locked up in a Leytonstone police station as a young boy as part of a cruel trick played by his father? As time has passed, many apparently authoritative accounts of Hitchcock's early life have been called into question. So from the start, we were clear that this was to be about imagining and not simply documenting Hitchcock's early life.

David combined some research on Hitchcock's immediate surroundings at the time he was living in first Leytonstone and then Limehouse, with an interest in the contemporary character of both areas, embracing a psychogeographical approach (trying to tap hidden histories of place) and making use of the situationist technique of the *dérive* (aimless wandering) to explore the territory. After experimenting with a series of images making direct reference to Hitchcock's apparently traumatic schooling at St Ignatius College in Stamford Hill,

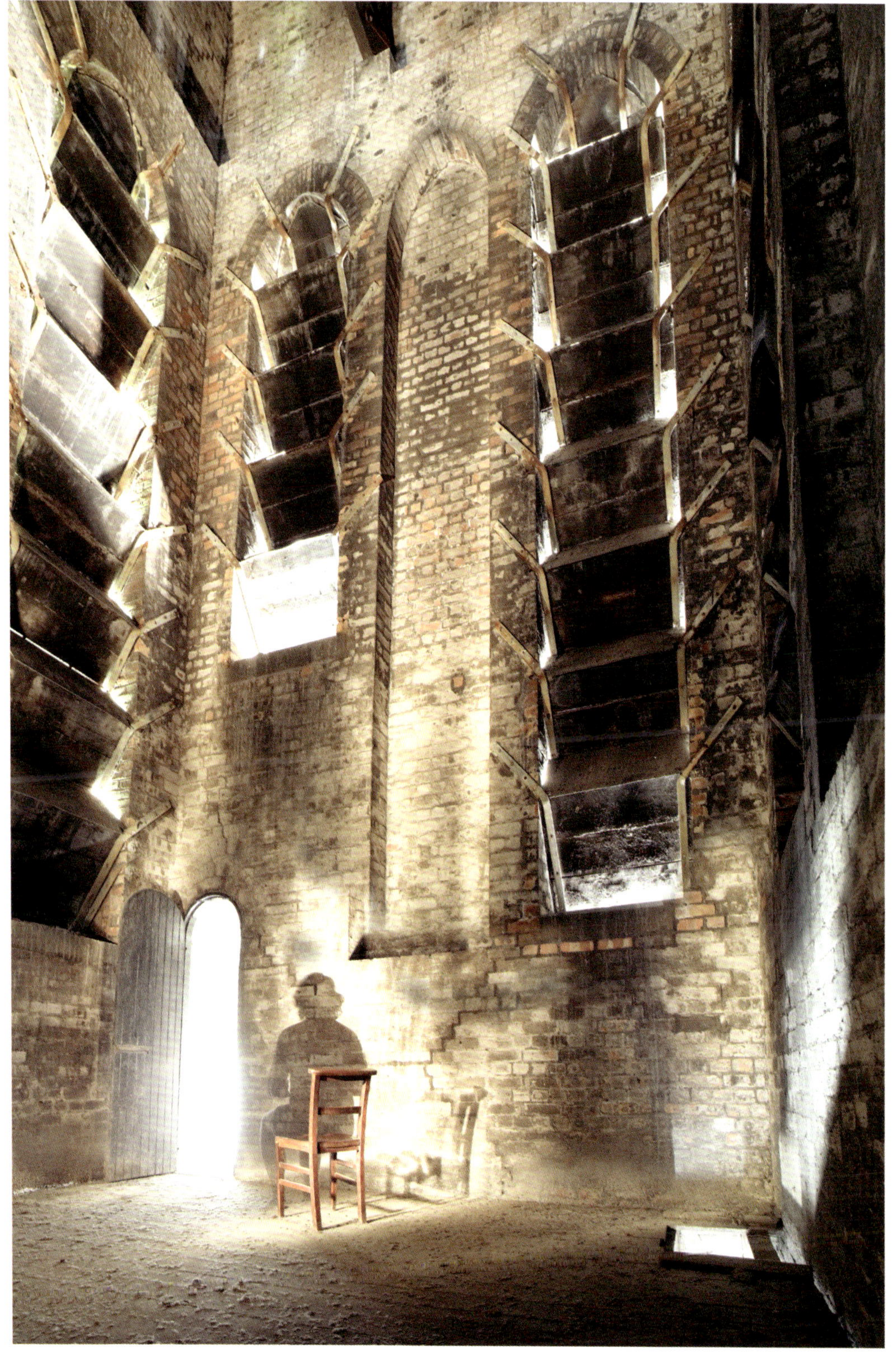

Spencer Rowell, St Ignatius Church, Stamford Hill, 2011.

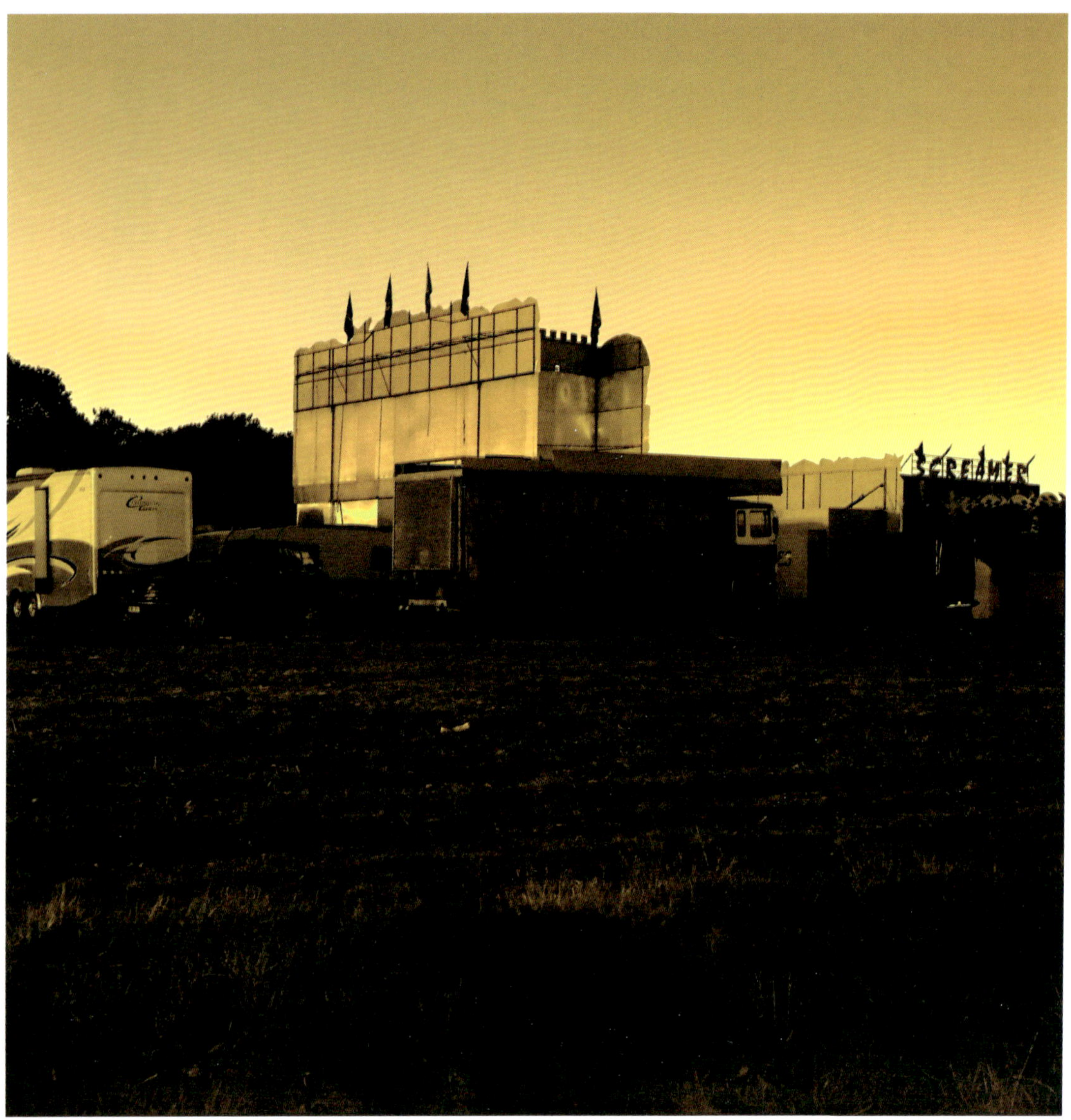

David George, *Screamer*, 2011.

Spencer subsequently took the more radical step of refusing all direct reference to records of Hitchcock's life or his films and instead produced a series of images in which he imagined himself as Hitchcock in an East End domestic interior, taking in his first preverbal impressions of the world and registering it as fearful, threatening, claustrophobic, pressing in from strange angles.

From the start, the project was conceived as a contribution to The Cass East End Archive with a linked symposium which took place on 24 November 2011, and which explored the issues arising from the project. The symposium was interdisciplinary, featuring an art historian, a theatre director, a psychotherapist, two photographers and a film studies specialist. When placing these images in the context of an archive of East End photography a number of factors became apparent. Firstly, the images would make a stark, and perhaps welcome, departure from the tradition of documentary photography so closely associated with the area. These images leaned towards a kind of fictional photography where the point of departure may be the real world but the contribution of the imagination is nevertheless paramount. Secondly, in so doing it would challenge the still dominant association between the archival and the documentary record by proposing that an archive might just as profitably concern itself with imaginings as with actual occurrences (under imaginings we can group such impulses as fantasies, memories, fears and desires). Thirdly, it would register the increasingly blurred boundaries around the idea of the East End, always more of an imagined space than a coherent geographical entity. Lastly, the project provided a means of registering the presence of Alfred Hitchcock (still sometimes referred to as the world's greatest film director) as a product of the East End itself (partly through his actual association with Limehouse but more importantly, as someone who astutely exploited the image of a dark, mysterious place where horror erupts in the midst of daily life in his films).

The East End has built up a formidable reputation as a repository for fears of many kinds. One plausible explanation for this ever-present sense of threat or danger may be the concentration of immigration, poverty and associated social ills such as prostitution in the East End, which gradually came to national consciousness through the nineteenth century.[1] Congregationalist minister Andrew Mearns eloquently summed up perceptions of the East End in the mid-to-late nineteenth century when he wrote that "seething in the very centre of our great cities, concealed by the thinnest crust of civilisation and decency, is a vast morass of moral corruption... [where]... incest is common, and no form of vice causes surprise or attracts attention."[2] Chinatown in Limehouse, where opium was freely available and vicious gangs fought each other, was particularly fertile material for writers such as Arthur Conan Doyle, Oscar Wilde and Sax Rohmer, seeking a stereotypical orgy of drugs, decadence, vice and corruption.

In an echo of the East End's problematic and controversial relation to the market driven policies of Margaret Thatcher, the East End of the mid-nineteenth century proved to be something of a test case for the ideas of free trade espoused by Richard Cobden. The novelist Jack London described the East End as a hellhole where "everything is helpless, hopeless, unrelieved and dirty".[3] Then, as now, free market capitalism not only rewarded winners and punished losers, it also required that there must be plenty of workers poor and desperate enough to work for very low wages so there was some incentive to keep people in poverty, as well as to lift them out of it. Cultural historian Ed Glinert refers to the Victorian East End as a "horrific afterbirth of the industrial revolution".[4] Then, as now, the rising middle classes could be callous and bullish about the poor.[5] Perhaps because they remained fearful of the social disorder consequent on social inequality, which they imagined might destroy their material gains.

Although daily life for many inhabitants of the East End may have been usually uneventful and far from the sensationalism favoured by the press and guardians of public morality, there were nevertheless sporadic and widely reported incidents during the first half of the twentieth century which led to the impression that the East End was a powderkeg of social unrest. The Sidney Street siege in 1911, the docker's strike of 1936 and the march of

Oswald Moseley's fascist Blackshirts in 1936 all helped to cement the impression that the East End was overrun by radicals and contributed to a sense of fear and anxiety, especially among the newly established middle classes whose social status was still precarious. The East End had also been the scene of horrific outbreaks of violence. Stories of Spring Heeled Jack, the Ratcliff murders, Jack the Ripper, gangster families such as the Bessarbians and the Kray Twins terrified many and have captured the imagination of the public for generations.

By all accounts, Hitchcock was an anxious and fearful person from a young age. He belonged to that class of newly prosperous business people seeking to consolidate their wealth with a social status, which still eluded them. As Anglo-Catholics, the Hitchcocks were further marginalised from respectable society. Yet Hitchcock's response to the specific and generalised anxieties he grew up with was to find a way to capitalise on them, to turn fears into entertainment.

The thriller form, now indelibly associated with Hitchcock, grew up with new forms of entertainment such as the amusement park which offered the public fear inducing rides on ferris wheels, bumper cars, water slides and other unsettling delights. It is in the amusement park that the link between screaming and laughter is most obviously seen.

Hitchcock found the opportunity to exploit fun fairs on many occasions, perhaps most memorably in his 1950 film *Strangers on a Train*, where the killer stalks his prey through the dark tunnel of love and murders her on Love Island, filmed in the reflection of her fallen glasses, one of the director's most perversely beautiful cinematic moments.

The German word *"angstlust"*, 'pleasure in fear', perfectly expresses the dynamic that Hitchcock exploits in his cinema, one which he owes to the work of German filmmakers. Hitchcock took many of his ideas from the German and Russian cinemas. From the German cinema, he learned about Expressionism through the films of Murnau and especially, Fritz Lang. Expressionism is commonly considered an outgrowth of the longer and broader German gothic tradition. Gothic art depicted a world of fear, foreboding and irrational superstition, which was nevertheless shown by artists as somehow more interesting and exciting than the common sense world.

The image opposite, which refers to visual motifs featured in Hitchcock's films, plays on the contemporary overlap of two traditions: the archive and the cabinet of curiosities. Both are concerned with bringing diversity into unity and both rely on the curator to propose an organising principle. It has been noted that the cabinet of curiosities relies on the dreamlike power of childhood and frequently the lure of the gothic.[6]

Hitchcock's own appetite for the gothic was undoubtedly piqued by stories of Jack the Ripper and his own proximity to the East End locations where the murders were committed. Hitchcock understood the way in which the media had told and retold the story in order to create fear among the public and capitalise on this. He experienced the drive to explain the murders in the media.[7] He also understood the way in which history and geography can be used to create what the Russian literary critic Bakhtin called a "chronotope", the place where "the knots of the narrative are tied and untied", creating in the case of his 1926 film *The Lodger* a "tale of the London fog" which nevertheless has a concrete and detailed grounding in London social life of the time.[8] With typical narrative economy, Hitchcock has made us share the fear of the public in this film (through German expressionist visual images, showing fog drenched streets and a string of fearful visages) as well as laying bare the ways in which fear is amplified, distorted and capitalised upon by the mass media (using the methods of Russian montage). The film also demonstrated Hitchcock's ability to see London locations through a glass, darkly.

London locations were often central to Hitchcock's work. The producers of *Sabotage*, 1936, proudly claimed that it would feature "more of the real London than any film yet made".[9] In his book *The Wrong House: The Architecture of Alfred Hitchcock*, Steven Jacobs makes a persuasive case that

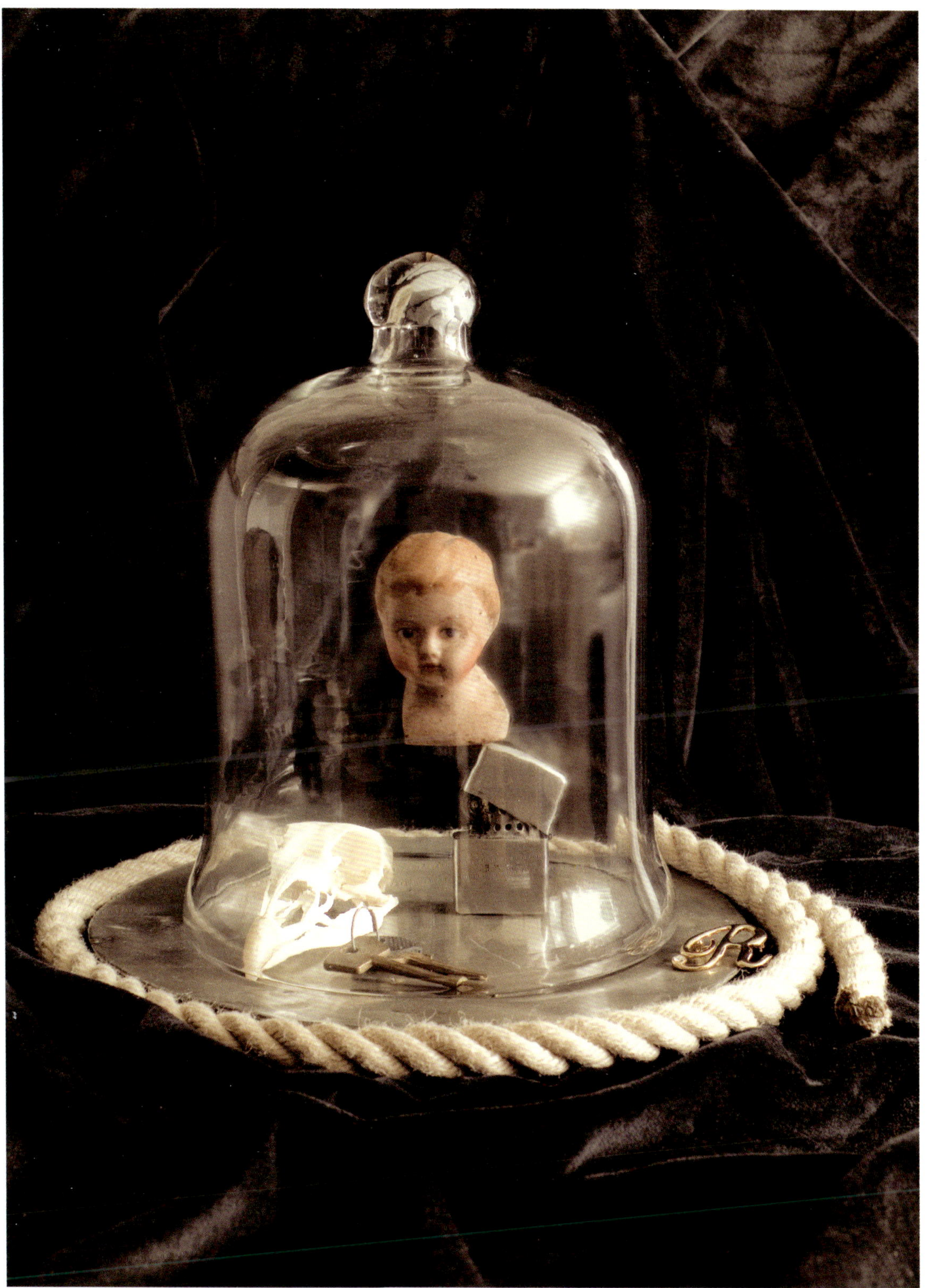

Nicholas Haeffner, *Hysterical Symptoms: Objects of Threat and Betrayal*, 2013.

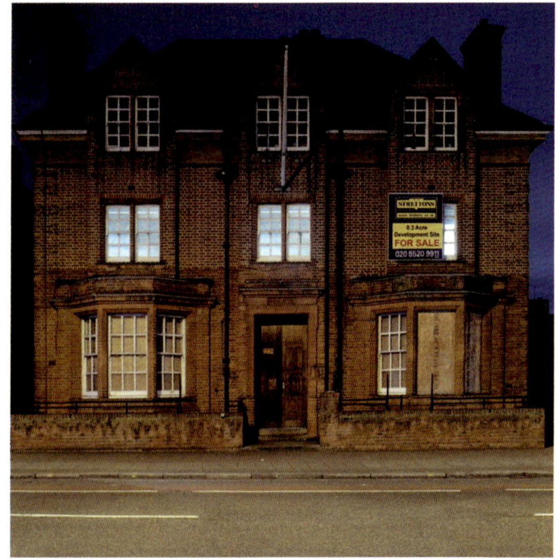

David George, Police station, Leytonstone High Street, 2011.

Hitchcock's films need to be understood more from the point of view of the role played by built environments.[10] Noting that Hitchcock was meticulous in his attention to locations, Jacobs shows us how important locations, monuments, houses and their interiors were to his films.

Jacobs observes that "Hitchcock presented the physical world as a dark, frightening, violent, unstable place, which is often a projection of a disturbed person shown through striking set designs and lighting effects as well as subjective camera shots."[11] In addition, "Hitchcock... often used narratives with characters that are determined, frightened or suppressed by their architectural environments."[12] While the gothic is given a new architectural location in Hitchcock's films: "instead of haunted castles, gruesome events take place in a suburban house, a sanitary motel bathroom, or a farm kitchen."[13] In fact, "virtually all of Hitchcock's films deal with the idea of the home".[14] But in Hitchcock's work "the house [is] a place of secrets and concealment".[15] Where did these anxious imaginings come from? An obvious answer would be from his childhood.

Hitchcock frequently repeated the story that he had been imprisoned as a young boy on the instructions of his father as a joke. The story was that the boy had been sent to a local police station at the age of six with a sealed note to give to the officer on duty. On reading the note, the officer promptly locked the little boy up in a cell until his father came to collect him. Both the officer and the father apparently found this amusing while Hitchcock recalls the event as a traumatic moment, which might offer some explanation for the omnipresent atmosphere of fear in his later films. However, if Hitchcock was actually around six years old at the time of the event and if he was incarcerated at the police station on Leytonstone High Street, as is widely believed, there is a problem: the police station on Leytonstone High Street was not built until some four years after the event was supposed to have taken place. There are many possible explanations for this conundrum. Perhaps it was another police station in the area at the time that the event took place. Perhaps the event took place later than Hitchcock remembers (he is vague and inconsistent about exactly when it happened). Or perhaps it never happened at all, and the story was concocted by Hitchcock as a convenient answer to the incessant questioning of journalists, all wanting to know the key to Hitchcock's work. So how should the rather photogenic old police station be presented as a photograph? If it is presented as a document, what

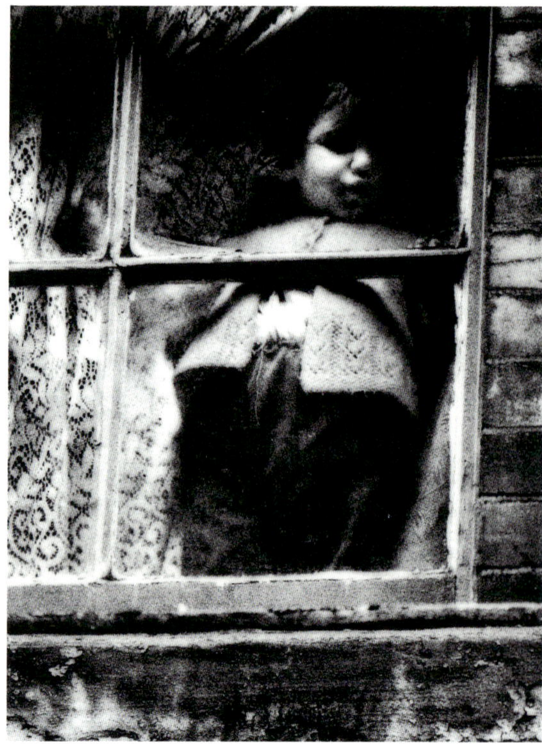

John Claridge, *Child at window*, E2, 1962.

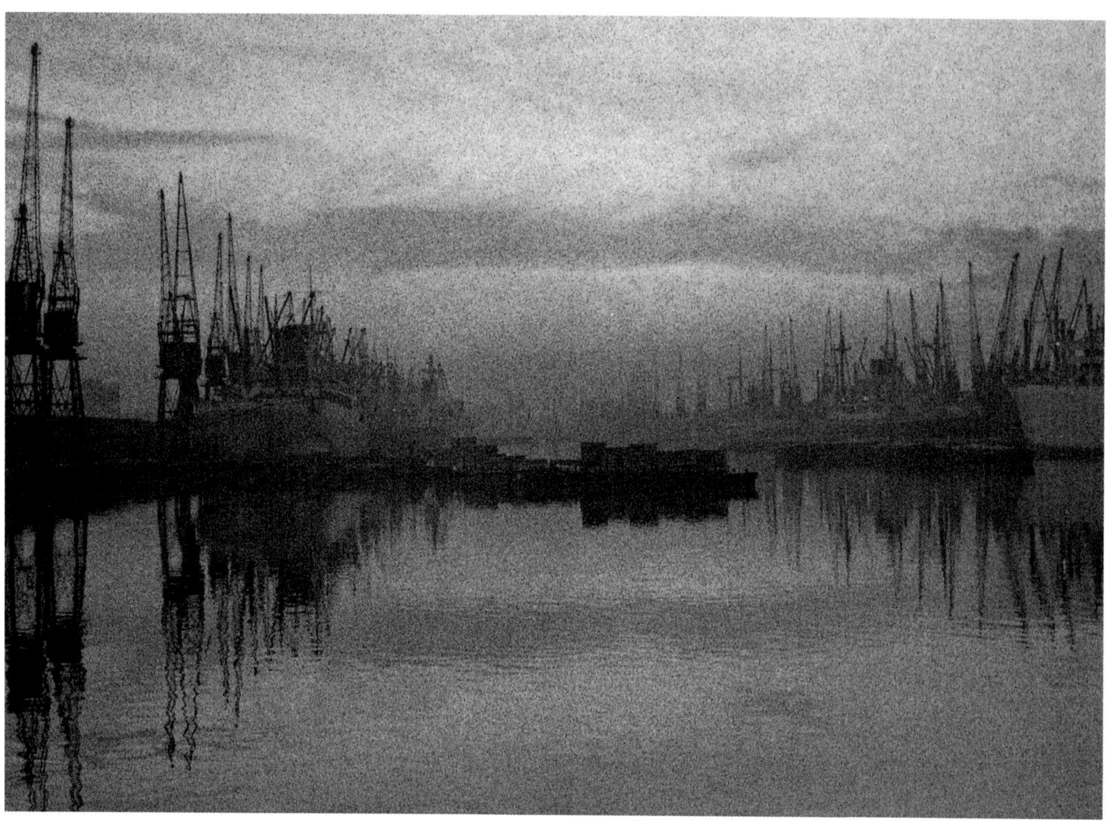

John Claridge, *London Docks*, E16, 1964.

is it documenting? Hitchcock's unreliable memory, our own lack of knowledge or his overactive imagination? One route through this territory is to take the idea of the photograph as a document and give it an expressionistic, slightly gothic spin as David George has done in his dreamlike, but hyperreal and extraordinarily detailed image.

There is plenty of precedent for such poetic and surreal images of the East End. For instance in the work of John Claridge.

What is being archived here? Not a factual document but an impression, a myth, a memory, a fantasy and perhaps a desire. The images are expressionistic. Expressionism can be characterised as an emotional (as opposed to a strictly representational) landscape. Often this is seen as a 'fantasy' landscape, as opposed to a 'real one'. Yet this opposition is plainly inadequate. The present is always already mediated by our memories of the past, which are partly imagined and always coloured by our emotional states.

Developments in contemporary photographic practice have seen some photographers move away from documentary representations of the sufferings of distant others (through images of war, famine and political oppression). Instead, apparently known and familiar subjects, such as oneself, one's friends, lovers and immediate environment are shown as suddenly problematic and strange (we could cite, for example, photographers as diverse as Sally Mann, Cindy Sherman, William Eggleston and Gregory Crewdson). The experience that documentary photography once set out to encapsulate has now come to be seen as no longer immediate in the first place, but rather mediated by memory, fantasy, history, culture and desire well before the camera intervened between the photographer and the world. Photography, which we are constantly reminded means writing with light, can quickly and easily mediate primal states of anxiety because it is also about writing within a dark space.

Like Hitchcock's films, photography has been studied by psychoanalytic critics who look for

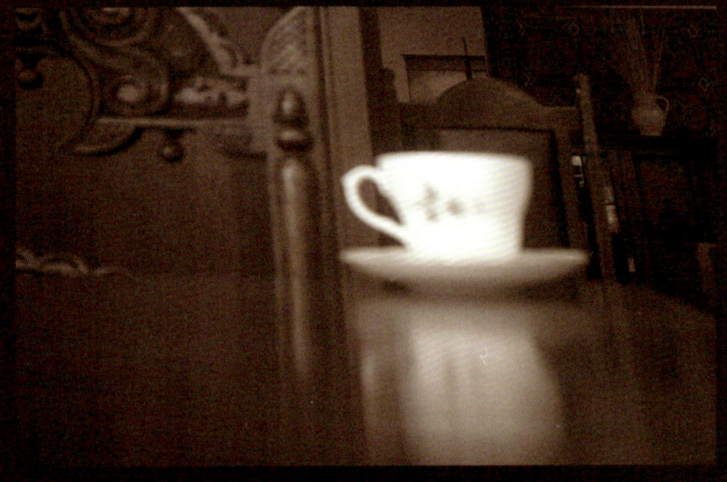

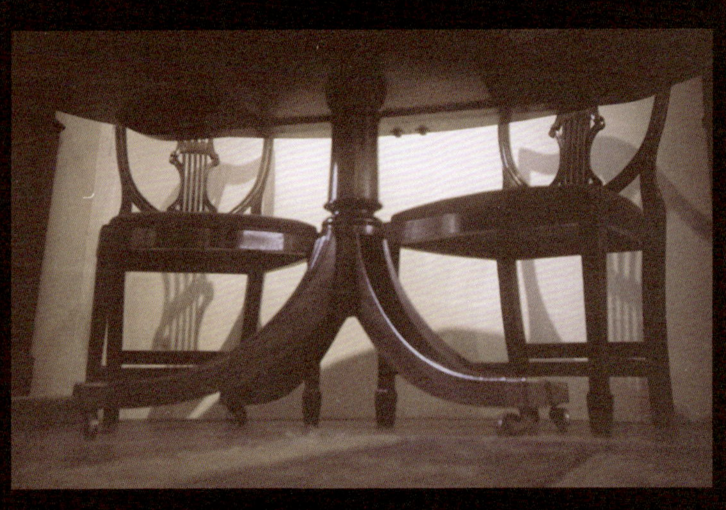

Oedipal narratives, sexual symbolism and fear of the feminine. In Freudian psychoanalysis, the concept of fear is replaced by the terminology of phobia, the cause of which is a repressed memory or wish.

Some of the photographs in *Shadows of Doubt* may be understood through Freud's central ideas. Many people now believe, as Freud urged us to, that childhood contains the key to the understanding of adult life and of artistic expression. Hitchcock's biographers have done much to encourage the belief that his childhood can explain his adult work (although this approach can also be reductive and misleading).

Spencer Rowell's images produced for *Shadows of Doubt* avoid any direct reference to Hitchcock's films or to specific stories about his childhood. Instead, the images evoke an atmosphere that is at once generic and at the same time uncannily redolent of Hitchcock's work. It is as if the cumulative effect of Hitchcock's films has been condensed into (and displaced onto) a nonspecific *mise-en-scène* of domestic unease, seen from the perspective of a small person.

Rowell took these images after abandoning a more dutiful attempt to illustrate specific facts and legends of Hitchcock's early life. Instead, the photographer got down on his hands and knees, and crawled around a domestic interior taking photos armed only with an old Box Brownie camera. Perhaps Hitchcock would have approved, since he made no bones about the delight he took in placing his actors in undignified situations, arguing that too much poise and self-control was inimical to the uncomfortable emotions he wanted to explore in his films.

Opposite: Spencer Rowell, 2011.

1. See, for example, Palmer, Alan, *The East End: Four Centuries of London Life*, London: John Murray, 2000 and Walkowitz, Judith, *City of Dreadful Delight: Narratives of Sexual Danger in Late-Victorian London*, London: Virgo, 1992.

2. See Palmer, *The East End*, p. 88.

3. Quoted in Glinert, Ed, *East End Chronicles* Harmondsworth: Penguin, 2005, p. 1.

4. Glinert, *East End Chronicles*.

5. See especially *Hard Times* by Charles Dickens for a bitter satire on the brutal materialism of the new propertied classes which remains as relevant today as it did when first published in 1854.

6. Davenne, Christine and Christine Fleurent, *Cabinets of Wonder*, New York: Abrams, 2011.

7. Allen, Richard, "The Lodger and the Origins of Hitchcock's Aesthetic" in *Hitchcock Annual* 2001–2002.

8. Bakhtin, Mikhail, *The Dialogic Imagination*, trans., Caryl Emerson and Michael Holquist, Austin: Texas University Press, 1985, p. 250

9. Krohn, Bill, *Hitchcock at Work* London: Phaidon, 2000, p. 24.

10. Jacobs, Steven, *The Wrong House: The Architecture of Alfred Hitchcock*, Rotterdam: 010 Publishers, 2007.

11. Jacobs, *The Wrong House*, p. 16.

12. Jacobs, *The Wrong House*, p. 21.

13. Jacobs, *The Wrong House*, p. 19.

14. Jacobs, *The Wrong House*, p. 32.

15. Jacobs, *The Wrong House*, p. 34.

A PALACE FOR US

TOM HUNTER
IN CONVERSATION WITH MICHAEL UPTON

MICHAEL UPTON How did the project come about?

TOM HUNTER From a commission from the Serpentine and Skills Exchange—which was a project to encourage artists and community groups to engage, and in particular for artists to get the elderly involved. Most of my work has involved highlighting and or raising awareness of issues related to marginalised groups in society and this was a similar one in that sense. I did a lot of research meetings, going to community groups. All the cast are from the estate. I was illuminating their story, creating a document of their narratives perhaps—not a straight documentary. They had what's called an "elders group". I met them. The project grew from there.

MU What was it about this particular group?

TH They were angry. It really wasn't what you might have expected. Old ladies sipping tea, sharing memories. These were a very vocal and opinionated group. And they had a wealth of information about the estate.

I spent three years visiting in six to eight week blocks. They had these three hour coffee mornings where I would have

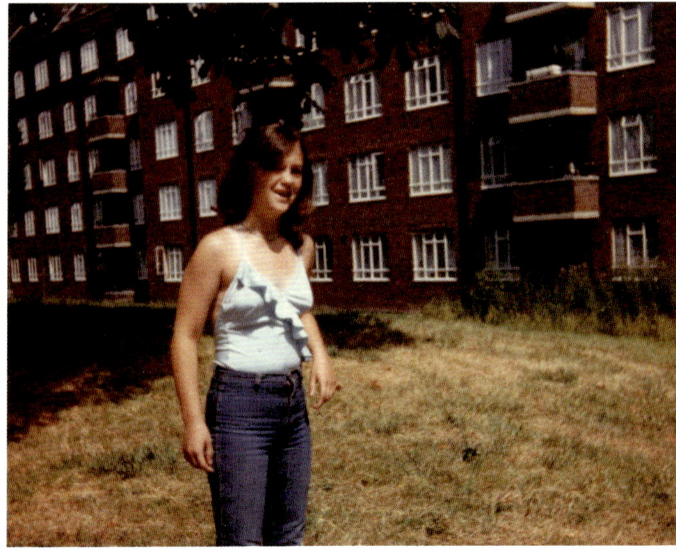

Images from family albums belonging to the residents of Woodberry Down.

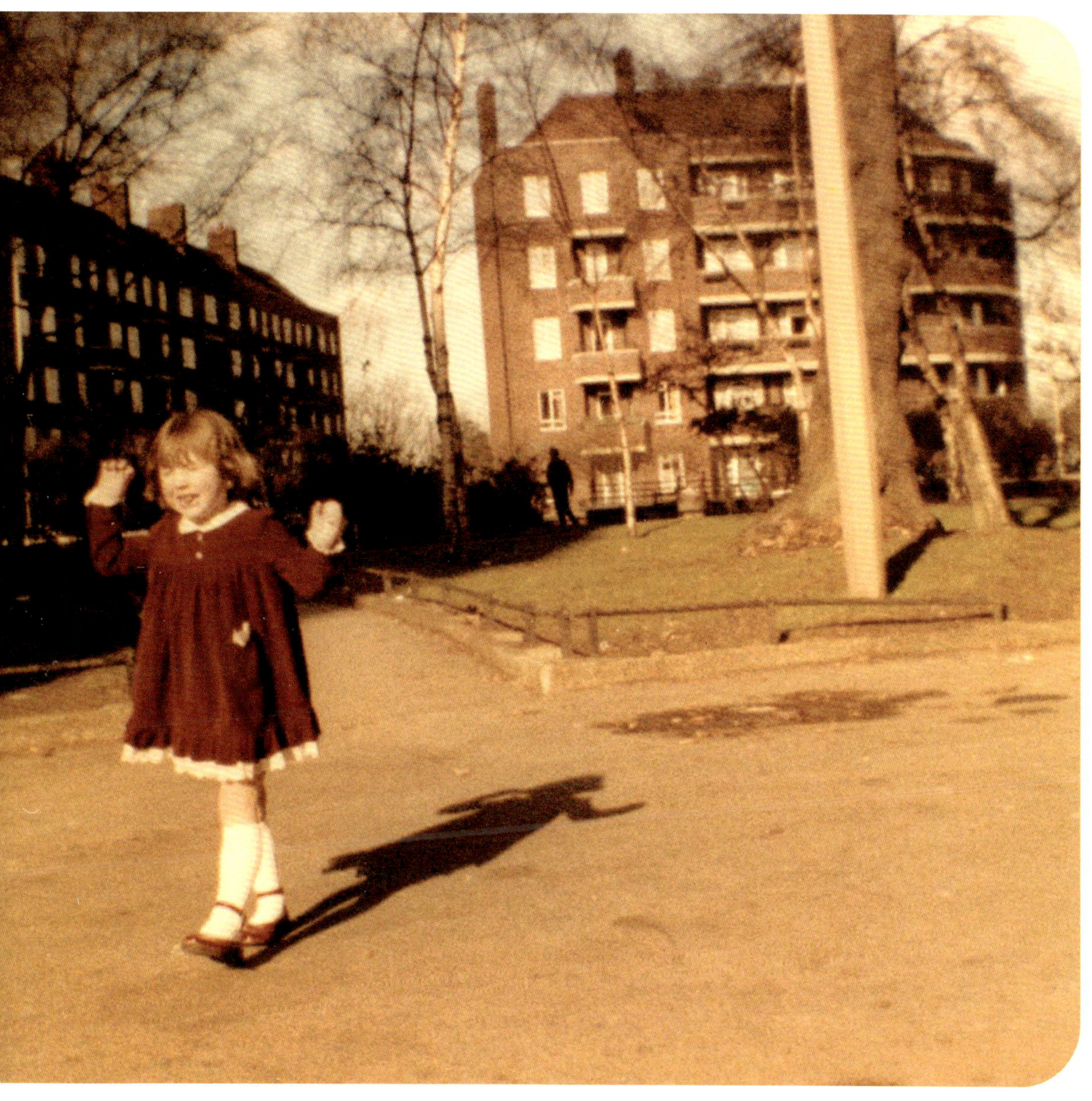

informal social chats and through these a detailed history began to emerge.... I began recording their stories, over two months I collected 25 oral histories.

One guy, Jim told a story. This woman, an air raid warden was out on the night of a bombing and heard that a house had been bombed. She realised it was her own and rushed from the scene to the shelter where she found her children safe. But her son didn't recognise her because in those few minutes where she feared her family were gone she'd gone grey—literally. Jim—who was telling the story—was the son. There was a lot coming out of these conversations about the war period—the bombing of course led to the requirement for social housing. You realised that this was where the welfare started, where a period of social housing started, out of this history of the blitz, out of the rubble.

There was this incredible pride in the project, this genuine dignity. As one of the participants said, "We couldn't believe it. We didn't have a home, and here it was it was a palace for us."

MU That relationship, the one between the personal and the political is a recurring theme for you.

TH From these stories you got the individual account but it revisited the way we see social housing. A big question mark hung over 1,100 flats and homes, but 4,000 more are needed—the story moved from "what happened" to "what's next" and the whole issue of social housing, the positives in there.

MU So was the intention from the start to make a film?

TH No. At first I took portraits of the Woodberry Down residents in their flats. But somehow they seemed flat. I think because I had heard the stories, I knew that the portraits didn't do them justice. I felt it needed to be developed in a different direction.

MU What was the process like—making a film and taking a still are quite different. I'm thinking about the things you've said in the past about a 'slow cooking' method of work....

TH Yes, it did require a change of 'headspace'.... I can take a year to get a picture, find a location, find the person, wait all day to get the shot, come back a different day because the weather isn't right, the light won't work. On a film, a shooting schedule has to be kept to. On the dance scene we had 60 people on set and we had to keep it to time and shoot on the day. It's a compromise in some ways, for a control freak. But it was exciting to work with a whole team of talented people.

MU In some ways that long three year build up of research visits was the equivalent of the 'slow cook' on the photographic work.

TH You could say that the film shoot was the equivalent of releasing the shutter. But it really was a team effort. I had to trust. And it worked.

MU I understand the film had a premiere at The Serpentine?

TH There was a Serpentine screening but the first screening was actually at the RIO in Dalston Kingsland—the nearest cinema to the Woodberry Down estate. We had the usherettes, the red carpet, free popcorn, the stars all sat in the front row and the place was packed with friends, family, local people. They were laughing and crying, seeing their stories told this way. There was a free dinner afterwards sponsored by Age Concern. The participants came to The Serpentine screening too, but the RIO one was the big moment. The response overall was incredible. People were really proud to have taken part, proud that members of their family had taken part. Because DVDs are relatively inexpensive it was widely circulated—people had their own copies and shared it with family.

MU Was this the first time you'd used 'found' images—these personal family photographs?

TH Yes. I have always loved photographs. And these are incredible documents, not necessarily any more 'true' a representation, but there's an innocence. This image (indicating girl in front of flats), she's so happy she's in the sun. The flats are in the background but they could be a street in a village or a Georgian town house, anywhere. The social housing is the backdrop but there's no sense of 'social housing' as an issue. I like the notion of what's documentary and what's fiction, of playing with that.

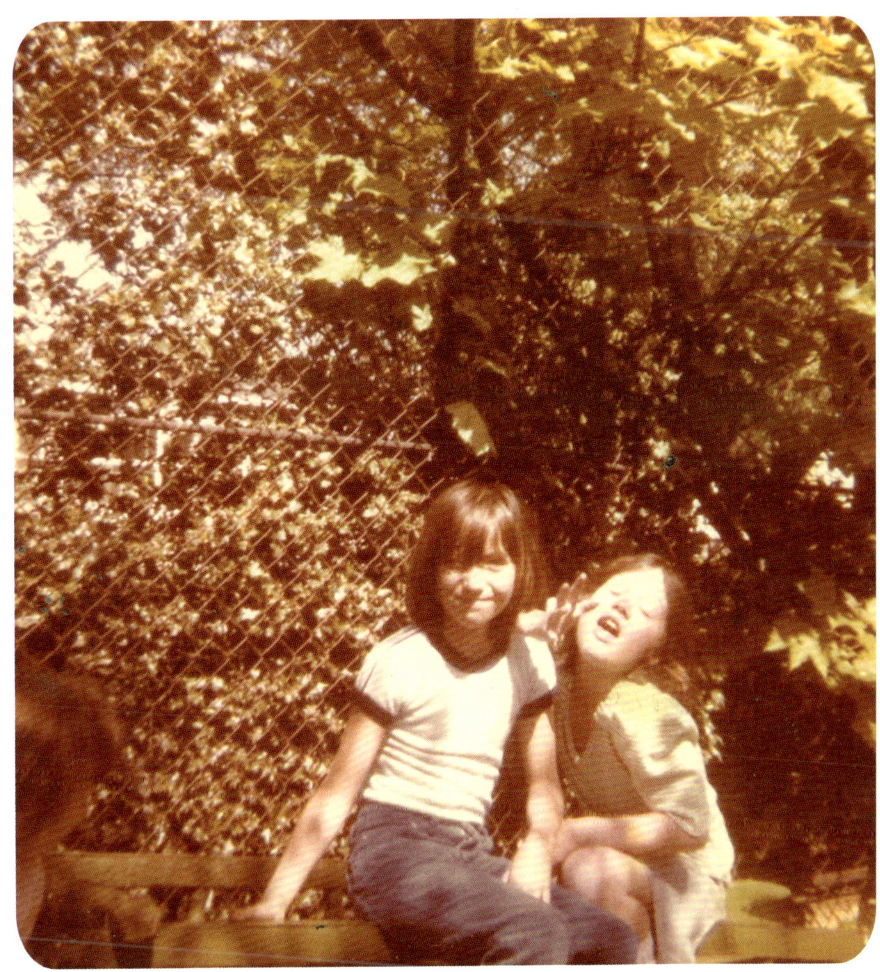

MU I can see that in your newspaper story inspired work such as *Halloween Horror*—the *Living in Hell* series, and the practice of combining classical influence and sensational content—or humanising the 'marginalised'.

TH Yes, in the film I am weaving in and out of that—a real image, a fake one, a performed scene—in the photographs the tension is within the frame.

MU This search for a 'real' East End, is there a real East End?

TH The whole history of the East End: its fables, myths, people, dockers, immigrants, poor, all of them are 'true' but separately they are caricatured, have become stereotypes. Our world is at once real and imagined—I play with notions of reality and artifice.

MU In *A Palace for Us* the stories reveal an East End sense of community, a shared sense of well being.

TH This was important for me in an age of 'Top Boy'.... I think this project demonstrates there is another side to social housing. From the war onwards, these many beautiful lives and moments.

MU You came from Dorset. Does being (or having been) an outsider to the East End make a difference?

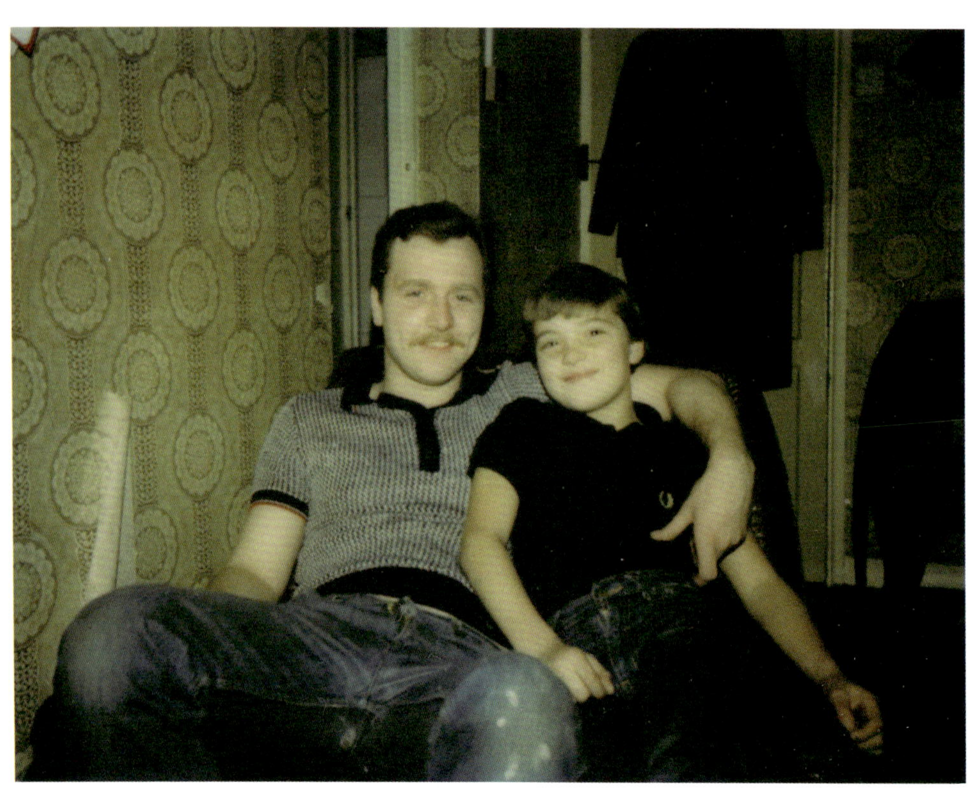

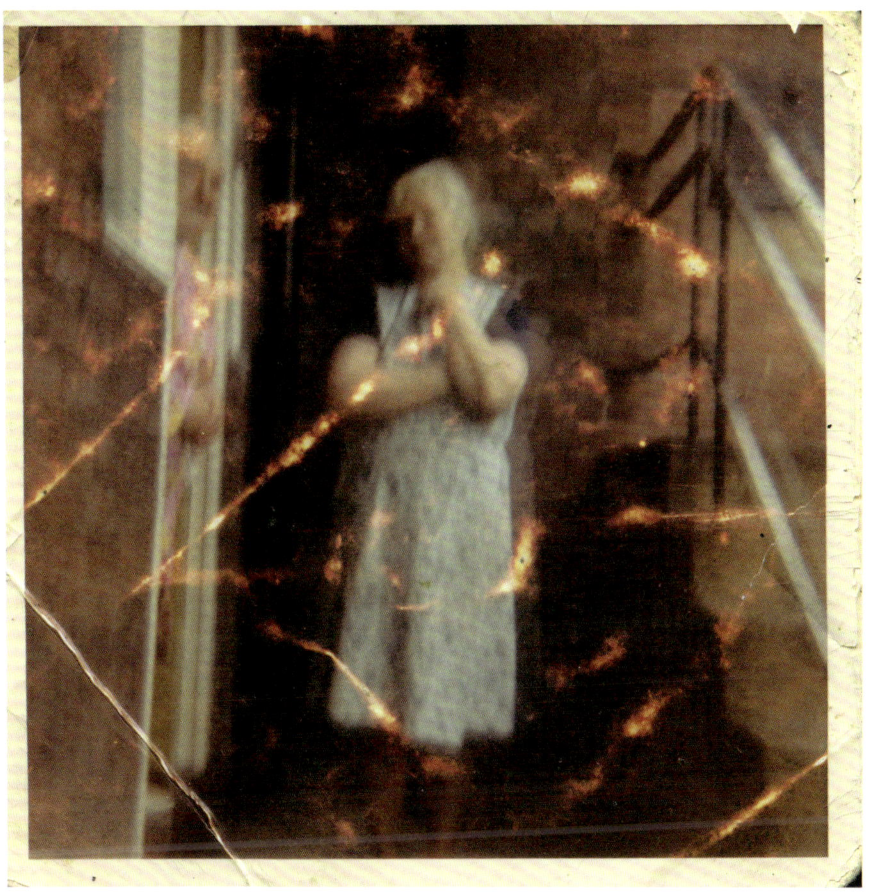

TH People often say to me "I've lived here for years but I've never seen it that way". Before I was here I had this image of a city—of things piled up, crammed together, the sort of Manhattan images of Magnum photographers. I came from a place where there was space, the sounds were wind and birds. When I go back I can't take photographs there, the big skies, the countryside and coast don't engage me.

MU Yet there is also sense of villages and the rural or some sort of 'arcadia' in some of your urban work.

TH The city is too big to understand. Too difficult to get your head round. One of the ways I've dealt with that is to make it my village, to imagine the village in the city. In a literal sense I have my pub, my shop, my fields. But it's also a way of understanding the city.

FOUND IMAGES

WORDS BY SUSAN ANDREWS

When the Geography department closed in what is now London Metropolitan University, David Wilkinson, a former member of staff from the Fine Art department, salvaged some large format photographic images from the skip. Subsequently, they sat in a box in his office until they were brought out during a discussion about the transformation of the local area. Many of the black and white negatives were scratched and the colour transparencies were faded (the now rosy colours would certainly not have been what the photographer intended nor what was seen when the images were first developed) but these altered photographic qualities contribute to a sense of the passage of time.

Initially, the authors of these found images were somewhat mysterious; "Brian", "Steve" and "Don" written in pencil on several of the negative sleeves suggested rather vaguely whom the photographers might be. However, it transpired that in the 1970s Don Shewan had been working in the Geography department at Queen Mary's College as a cartographer. Collaborating with two assistants, another cartographer Steve Pratt and Brian Canarens, a photographer, Shewan had been in the process of making an atlas of the East End and mapping social trends; there were huge and complex changes in the area with rising unemployment, factory closures, redevelopment and the start of the transformation of the Docklands. However, when Don Shewan began a

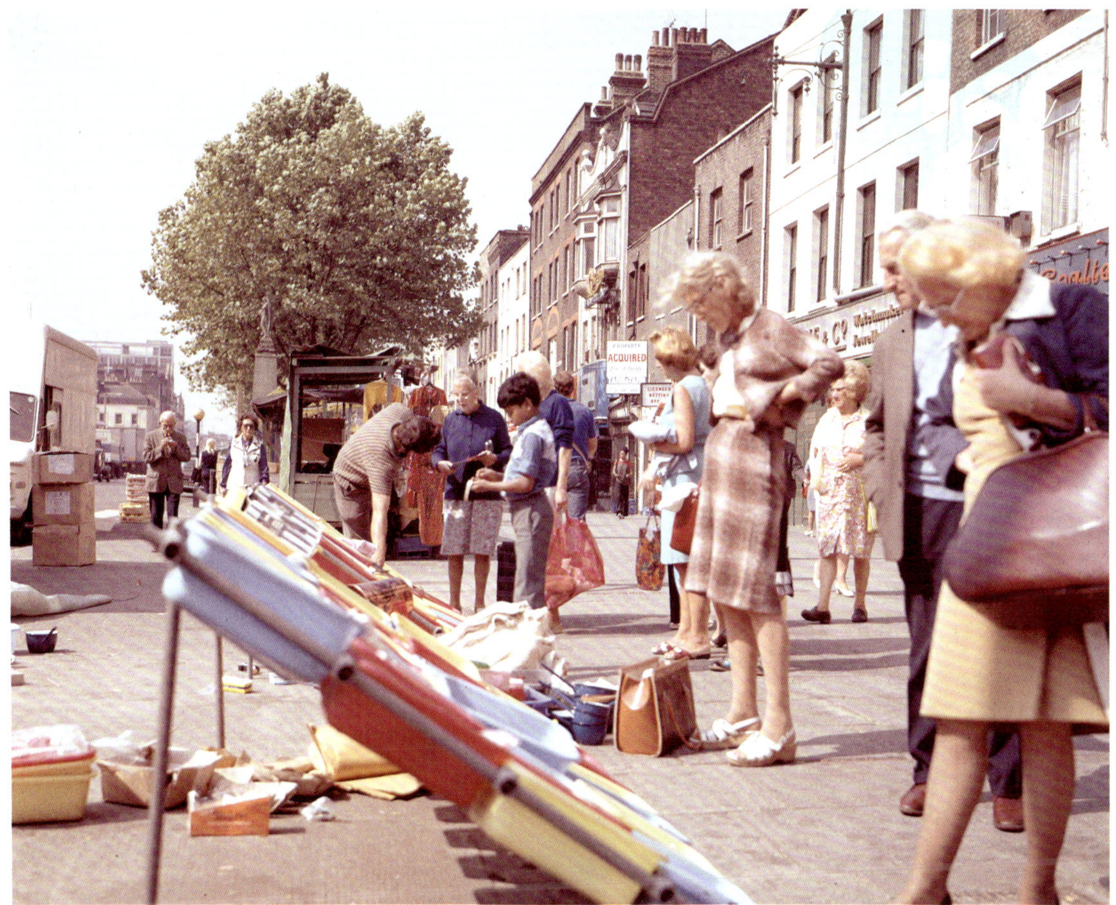

Found image, Whitechapel High Street, c. 1971.

new job at London Guildhall University (now the London Metropolitan University) the project did not progress and although he had kept the material for teaching purposes, when the department finally closed, many photographs were discarded.

This small, rescued collection now forms a part of The Cass East End Archive and, although not individually authored, the agenda for making the work is clear: to provide a social document of the time. In order to do this, the photographers chose to use an unwieldy 5x4 camera that requires a tripod and therefore a fixed position, the purpose of which must have been to clearly communicate the detail. In some photographs, however, a shallow depth of field obscures information and the edges of the frame reveal a less considered composition that is more concerned with the subject matter than any aesthetic consideration. From a contemporary perspective however, the foibles, flaws and damage contribute to the fascination these images hold as emissaries from another time, communicating a particular photographic approach and providing evidence of the social changes that have occurred in population, culture, fashion and architecture.

In the following section, the artist and writer David Howells makes a personal response to two of these photographs and reflects on the photographic and social issues they raise.

FOUND IMAGES—TUBBY ISAACS

WORDS BY DAVID HOWELLS

La forme d'une ville change plus vite, hélas, que le coeur d'un mortel.

Baudelaire, *Le Cygne*

The identity of the photographer is unknown to me, nor his or her purpose in taking the picture. In terms of genre it would certainly be considered a documentary image, and its exact location is quite familiar to me. But no other information attaches to it; apart from the stall—which explains itself well enough—there are no obvious signs as to what it is I should be looking at, or why. My purpose is not so much to look at the photograph as to inhabit it, if only for a few moments, in which case the less I know of such things the better.

I could be standing there with the photographer, a few feet away from the stall. It is mid-afternoon, warm, probably summer—I know this from the shadows that fall across the pavement on my side of the street. The sky is a purple artefact of 1970s colour chemistry and has probably shifted in hue over the decades, but it is in any case impossible to verify such things. The colour of the sky almost exactly matches the printed floral pattern of the nylon dress that a middle-aged woman is wearing in the foreground. She is counting money out of a purse to pay for something, as another woman (they are both wearing white shoes) turns back towards her. They do not look like tourists and quite possibly live here, part of an ageing urban proletariat that still inhabits the city centre. Their children will have already moved to the suburbs.

On this afternoon the stall is doing steady business but the food itself is invisible, hidden behind the counter. Nor do the signs give much away: "F....s for Jellied Eels"; "We Lead Others Follow". Something hand-written and sellotaped in the window, but illegible, can be had for 25p. There is a bottle of vinegar at one end of the counter. Three men are standing, one at the counter in flared corduroys and two others either side of the stall, all with their backs turned, heads down. I imagine them to be eating some small and gristly stuff that requires a degree of concentration on their part. Having bought their takeaway food they haven't taken it very far, and still face as if in deference toward the stall. Perhaps they do so in order not to face each other, and are slightly ashamed of themselves. A canopy in red and white Punch and Judy stripes keeps a white-coated

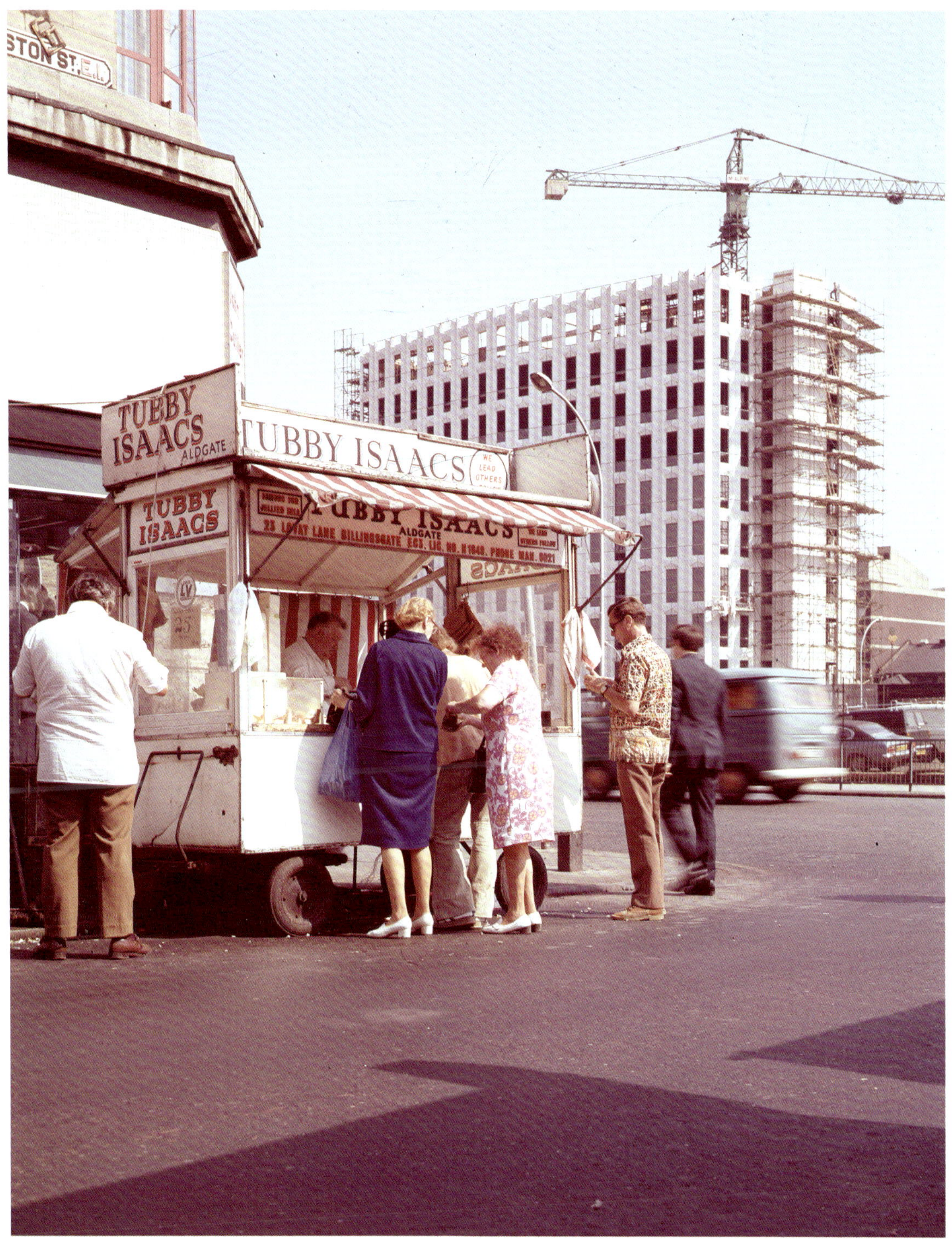

Found image, Tubby Isaacs stall, Goulston Street, c. 1972.

stall keeper—whom I hadn't noticed at first—in the shade at the back. He too busies himself with something that I cannot see, his eyes downcast.

A businessman in a suit is not even stopping at the stall, but walking fast along Whitechapel High Street, heading east out of the city. His left leg is dissolved in the motion of its step, as in the early daguerreotypes. The exposure, and the moment of the whole photograph, must be slightly longer than I had first appreciated, and time builds itself around this moment: enough time for the other six people and myself, but not for him. None of the group is interested in the picture that is being taken of them, or in my imaginary presence. It is quite probable that I already know more about them than they will ever notice of each other. But this knowledge cannot escape the confines of the photograph. When the few moments that it holds together are over at least six of them will walk away, and so will I.

Many things are less permanent than they appear to be. That stall still stands today in exactly the same spot, its territorial rights presumably guaranteed by some obscure and as yet unrepealed byelaw. But other things—streets and buildings and whole quarters of this city—will steal way as surely as these eel eating customers are about to. Tubby Isaacs' address is written over the counter of his stall: Billingsgate EC3. Billingsgate is the ancient site of a fish market at the Pool of London that will continue for another ten years before it is evicted to Poplar in 1982, and then somewhere even further over the horizon in the early 2010s. As the 1970s continue, 'markets' will become increasingly remote and abstract things with—paradoxically—more and more power over the lives of ordinary people. The stall is in fact a wheeled cart, as if it were meant to return whence it came each night, presumably pulled by its operator. But I have not known it to move from Goulston Street in 40 years, although it now faces competition from an adjacent burger stall—easier meat.

In the background of the photograph, on the other side of the main road, a new office building is under construction, recognisable as Beagle House, a modernist design of Richard Seifert—"the colonel" of London's post-war planning battles. It has recently been proposed for demolition, with approval from Tower Hamlets Borough Council. In 1971 the popular reaction to some of Seifert's more notorious projects—Centre Point, Euston Station—has not yet begun in earnest. The exterior is spanned by a technoid grid of interlocking modular cells; not inelegant, but the overall scheme is mediocre. For that reason Beagle House will probably escape the opprobrium but will not be missed, or even remembered, when it disappears again in 40-odd years' time.

The middle ground between the whelk stall and Beagle House is empty, save for the traffic moving rapidly past along Whitechapel High Street, and what must be a car park on the other side; the new building is actually further away than it appears to be. In 1971 the Aldgate road junction has recently been converted to a gyratory system, the last word in town planning following the publication of the Buchanan Report in 1963. For a post-war economy that can't actually afford much modern architecture, urban traffic systems knocked through nineteenth century cities offer a kind of modernity on the cheap. In 1971 all this is still new, and for a while, it even seems to work; the traffic is moving, after all. The Aldgate junction will eventually be restored to two-way traffic—Corbusier's "pack-horse way"—in 2009.

Some things are more permanent than they seem to be. The shadows that fall forwards across the street from where I am standing are strangely familiar. I now realise that they are cast by some temporary hoardings immediately behind the camera. Behind them, just over my shoulder, is an empty plot, site of the original Aldgate East tube station that was abandoned in 1938, damaged by wartime bombing and demolished in the 1950s. In 1971 the site is still derelict, and will remain so. It will be briefly cleared of trees and undergrowth, as if for redevelopment, just before the economic concept of unlimited growth comes to an end in the global financial crash of 2008. The plot behind the hoardings will then gradually return to a state of nature, a Piranesian sump colonised by ferns, rosebay willow herb, ivy, and other self-seeded flora.

I have now been staring at this scene for rather too long—possibly longer than any of the other human beings involved, including the photographer—and a strange thought has crossed my mind. I cannot be sure, but the mauve of the sky seems to have shifted again in hue—slightly further towards the red end of the spectrum. My memory for colour is unreliable, but I suspect the light in this photograph is still changing, slowing down. Like a receding galaxy, this and other colour photographs of the 1970s continue to send their light towards us, but with a marked colour shift that registers their distance and the velocity with which they retreat into the past. Eventually, as the generations die out that were still able to make contact with these images by an effort of imagination and memory, they will become history: still extant but invisible to the naked eye of a present tense.

It is time to stop: the light is weakening now and this moment has come to an end.

Overleaf: Found image, Wickham's Department Store, Mile End Road, c. 1971.

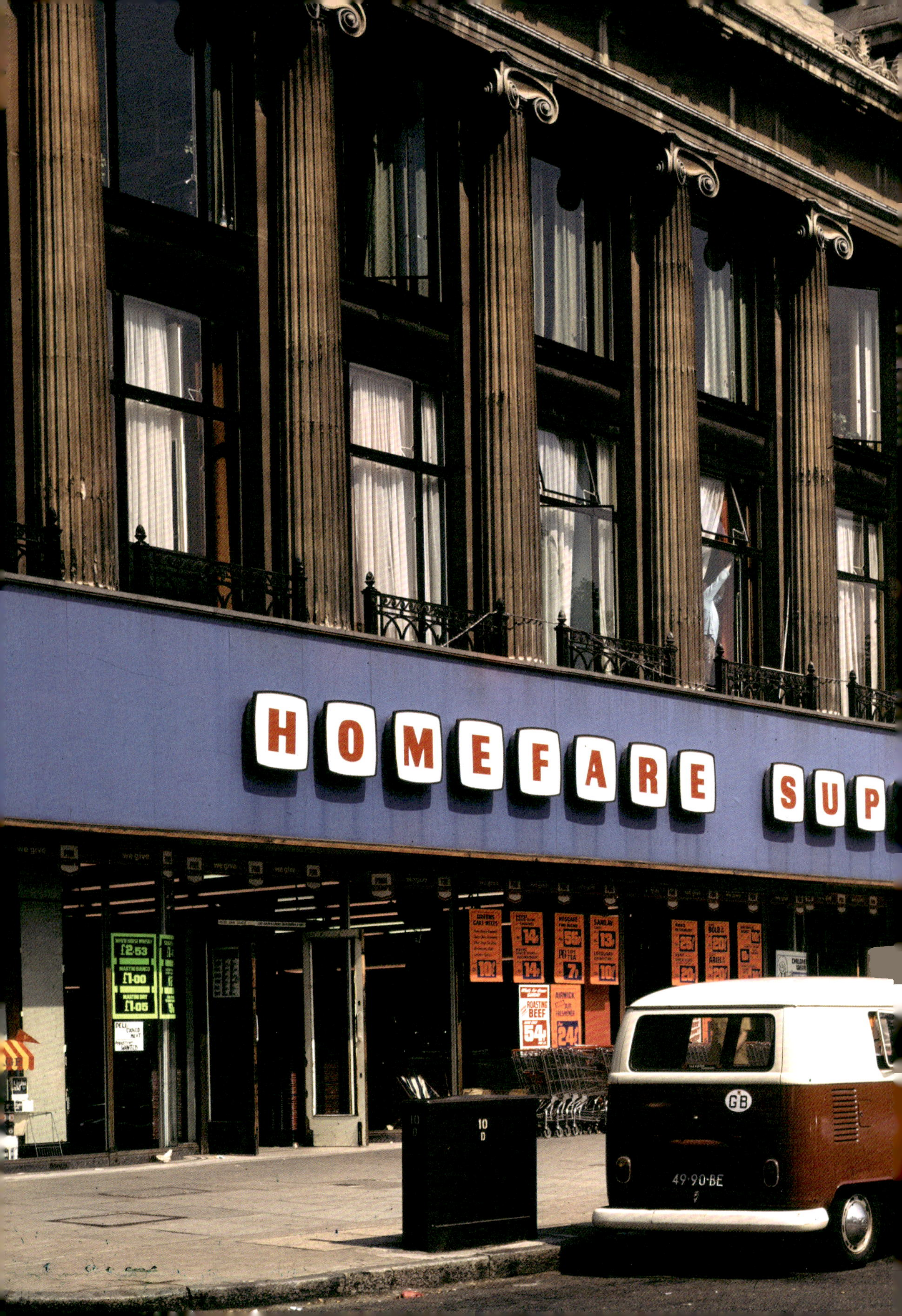

HOMEFARE SUP
£2·53
£1·00
£1·05
ROASTING BEEF
54
AIRWICK
24
10 D
GB
49·90·BE

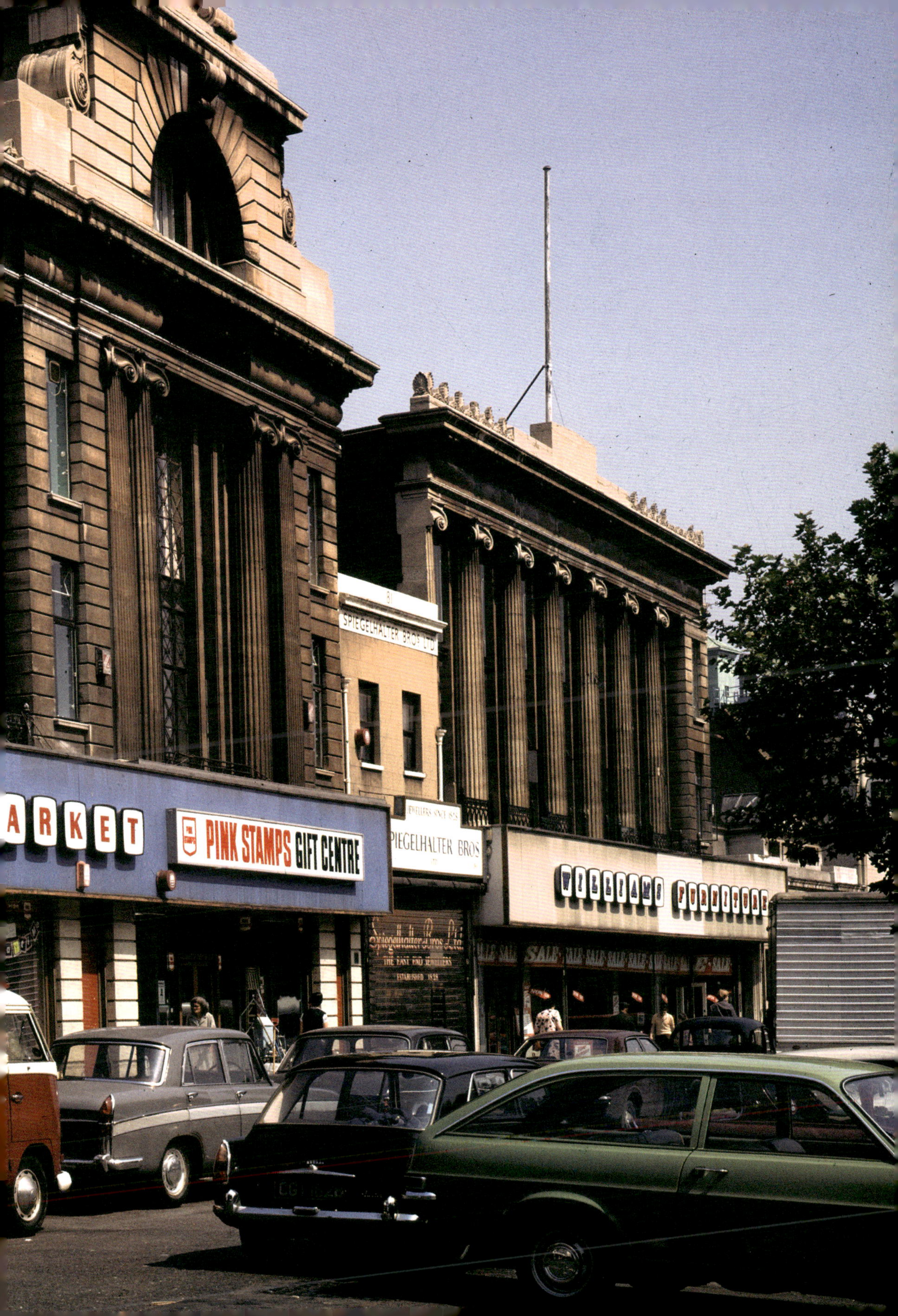

ARKET
PINK STAMPS GIFT CENTRE
81
SPIEGELHALTER BROS LTD
JEWELLERS SINCE 1828
PIEGELHALTER BROS
Spiegelhalter Bros Ltd
THE EAST END JEWELLERS
ESTABLISHED 1828
WILLIAMS FURNITURE
SALE

FOUND IMAGES—WICKHAM'S DEPARTMENT STORE

WORDS BY DAVID HOWELLS

The present order is the disorder of the future.
Attributed by Ian Hamilton Finlay to Louis Antoine de Saint Juste

I am looking at this photograph in order to solve a problem. Since it is a problem of appearances, the photograph presents both the problem and the only prospect of a solution. It is of a commercial building that I have not once entered, despite having walked past it many times over 30 years. But this photograph has recorded something that I had never noticed (which is why I am still looking at it now): that the building is incomplete, interrupted approximately two thirds of the way along its length by a much smaller, shabbier construction, a sort of shack which occupies the gap in the facade without even matching its height. Rank visual inconsistency is a characteristic of London, and of its East End in particular, which in common with many of its inhabitants I have learned not to notice. If pressed, I will explain away such things in terms of the wartime bomb damage by which London continues to recognise itself, even in the twenty-first century. I will continue to say of the East End that it is damaged, as one would of a person injured beyond recovery, and keep walking. Photographs are different: they offer no escape from appearances and we cannot walk through them; we can only either look, or not look at all.

But in fact I'm quite wrong about the damage in this case, which is possibly the reason why the photograph was taken in the first place. The story of this building is locally famous: in the early twentieth century Wickham's department store was planned as a "Harrods of the East". Numbers 69 to 89 Mile End Road were acquired as a suitable site by the developers, with the exception of a jeweller's shop at number 81 that obstinately refused to sell up. In 1927 the Wickham family decided to start building anyway, on either side of the older property, perhaps expecting its owners to eventually capitulate, which however they never did. This arrangement survived the war intact, and at the time that this photograph was taken, Wickham's had already gone out of business, whilst the jewellers continued to trade and would do so for another decade. The two disjoint Wickham premises would henceforth be occupied by a series of separate and rather temporary businesses, and as of 2012 the chain stores Tesco Express and Sports Direct. Number 81 Mile End Road is now empty and derelict. It was the creative destruction of commercial forces—only briefly interrupted by the War—which produced this anomaly, and which continues to produce London's uniquely unfinished environment. The real mistake of its builders was to try to make something that looked like architecture. One has to leave the city altogether for some time, or see this process at work in a photograph, to see it at all.

I may know the story but the incompleteness of appearances still troubles me. A photograph is a superficial thing twice over: an accident of light by which one surface is caught upon another surface, a beautiful frozen mirror without substance. Buildings are substantial, but it is by their surfaces that they make themselves known. A classical facade—even in debased form—promises order and completeness, symmetry and the correct relationship between the whole and the parts, between cause and effect, all in a composition intended for a single point of view at one point in time. It is a form that anticipates the rectangular frame of the photograph itself.

In this least ideal of cities, such promises are soon broken. The photographer finds that he or she cannot set up the camera directly in front of the building: to do so would require standing in the middle of the Mile End Road, and already by the 1970s a mass of carelessly parked cars obscures the view at street level. The symmetry of the facade is in any case already broken, not by an accident of posterior history, but by a prior accident of design. The aesthetic of classical ruins, in which the symmetry of origins gives way to the asymmetry of fate, has become so familiar as to be reassuring, but this is a ruin in reverse. And on closer inspection, those Ionic columns aren't holding anything up at all; their feet do not even touch the ground and it is actually their weight that is being supported by a curtain wall structure in order to leave uninterrupted window frontage on the ground floor.

The photographer is not only recording this devaluation of appearances: he or she is helping to bring it about. As the population of photographs increases without limit, so will the importance of the image world in our experience of the city. We now expect buildings to look like photographs of themselves. By 1927 iron-based industrial building techniques had already destroyed the integrity of classical ornament, and although modernism was supposed to address that problem by embracing it, integrity itself was never in question. The twenty-first century expedient of 'facadism'—the preservation of a listed historic facade whilst demolishing the rest of the building for redevelopment—will bring about a much more radical dissolution of substance and accident, and future inhabitants of London will need no longer think of surfaces as concealing depths, or of exterior appearances as expressing an interior nature. The work of research to discover truth in a resistant physical substance, and the attendant archaeological habits of mind—too slow, too linear!—will have to be unlearned.

If I imagine this photograph as part of a sequence which will include all the photographs in the world, arranged somehow in the right order, it will make a kind of film of history. I know of course that this is an inadequate view of both history and photography, but it is one that I cannot easily give up. It is a history in which I should be able to see how buildings have been put up and taken down, how one style has replaced another, how villages have grown into cities, and cities into ruins in the course of empire. It is what the traveller in H G Wells' *The Time Machine* can see. That is what I'm trying to do now, looking at this photograph, but it isn't working; something right here in the film of history is broken; each time I come across it the film has to be stopped and then started again. I can only make sense of this image by inserting something, a kind of erratum: "for x read y". I must do this every time I look at it, and I am beginning to wish that I had never seen the photograph. It used to amuse me; now it irritates me.

The name of the jewellery business that is responsible for all this trouble can be read quite clearly in the photograph: it is *Spiegelhalter*, meaning 'mirror-holder' in German. The mirror-holders have long since fled the scene, but symmetry cannot be restored. I am now turning it upside down and back to front in my hands, trying to get behind the image, to see past it, to find something inside, beyond or before it. But I cannot, it will not yield anything more than what it appears to be. Besides, I have forgotten to mention something else about this photograph: that it is not a print but a transparency, a 'diapositive'; it has no other side.

RECOGNITION

HEATHER MCDONOUGH AND ROD MORRIS

These portraits are selected from two Photobooth events made by the photographers Rod Morris and Heather McDonough for the Museum of London and the Hackney Museum. The work was originally one of many projects undertaken by London Transport Museum for the exhibition Overground Uncovered: Life along the Line, where photographs were taken of people along the route of the six boroughs of the new London Overground extension.

Depicted here are people from the stations and local markets of Ridley Road Market, Dalston, Haggerston, Shoreditch, Canada Water and Brick Lane, Whitechapel. This process allowed the Museum to investigate how transport regeneration impacts on London and its people, exploring notions of identity and the shaping of communities. Subsequently, Hackney Museum commissioned the *Photobooth Project* to record the faces of Hackney residents at various public events as part of their *Mapping the Changes* project, shown at Hackney Museum 2012.

The photographers invited members of the public to pose for their portraits in a temporary photobooth, which utilised available light and a black backdrop to isolate the sitters from the chaos of city life. The work references the automated photobooth convention of direct head and shoulders shots, a mode particularly used formally for the purposes of identification. However, in this work there is no detached officialdom present; the details are clearer and sharper, and the images, frequently printed larger than life, reveal the sitters' humanity. Seen collectively, the portraits are not only indicative of demographic changes within the region but a celebration of the diversity of the communities they represent.

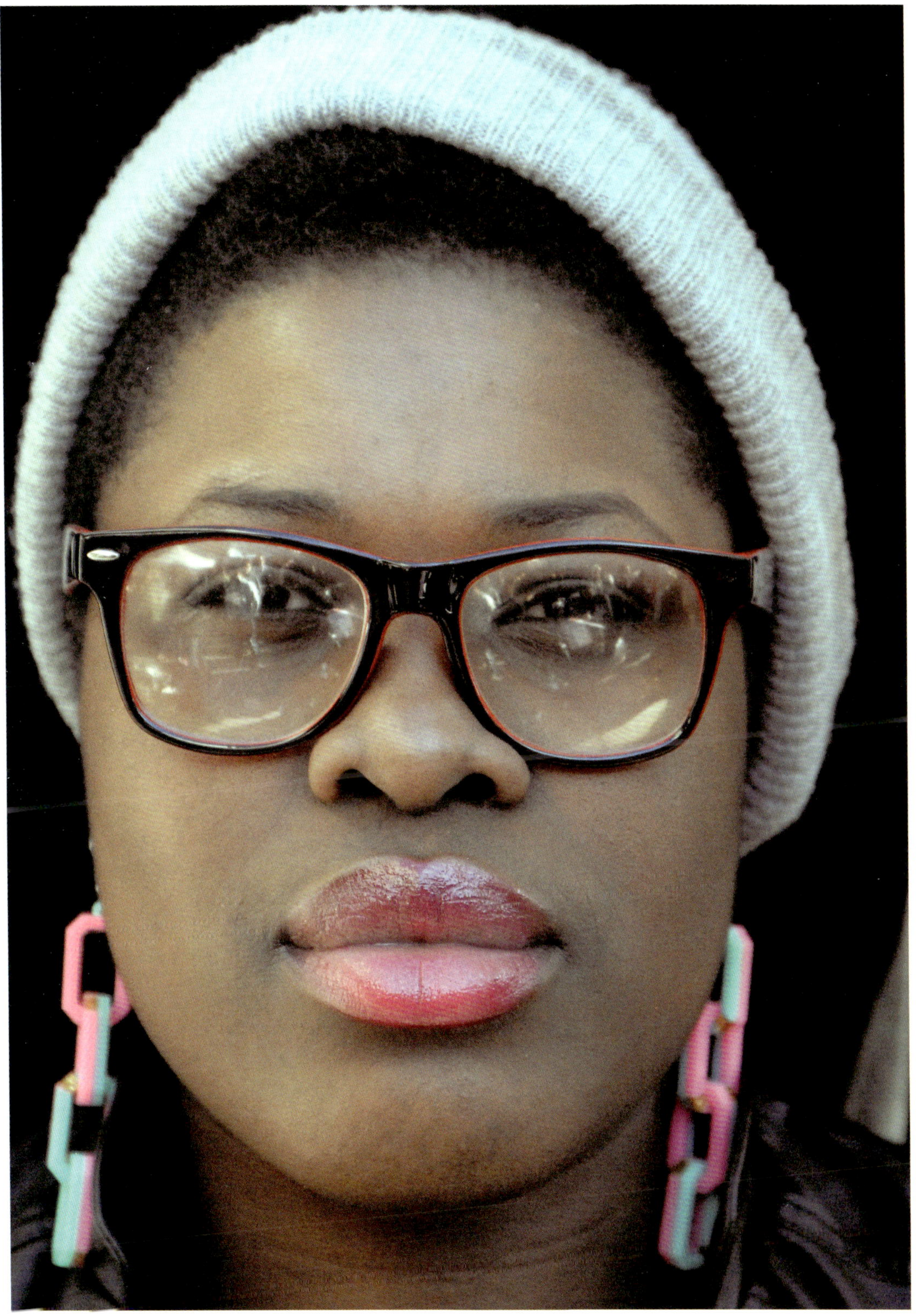

Above and overleaf: Heather McDonough and Rod Morris, from the series *Recognition*, 2011.

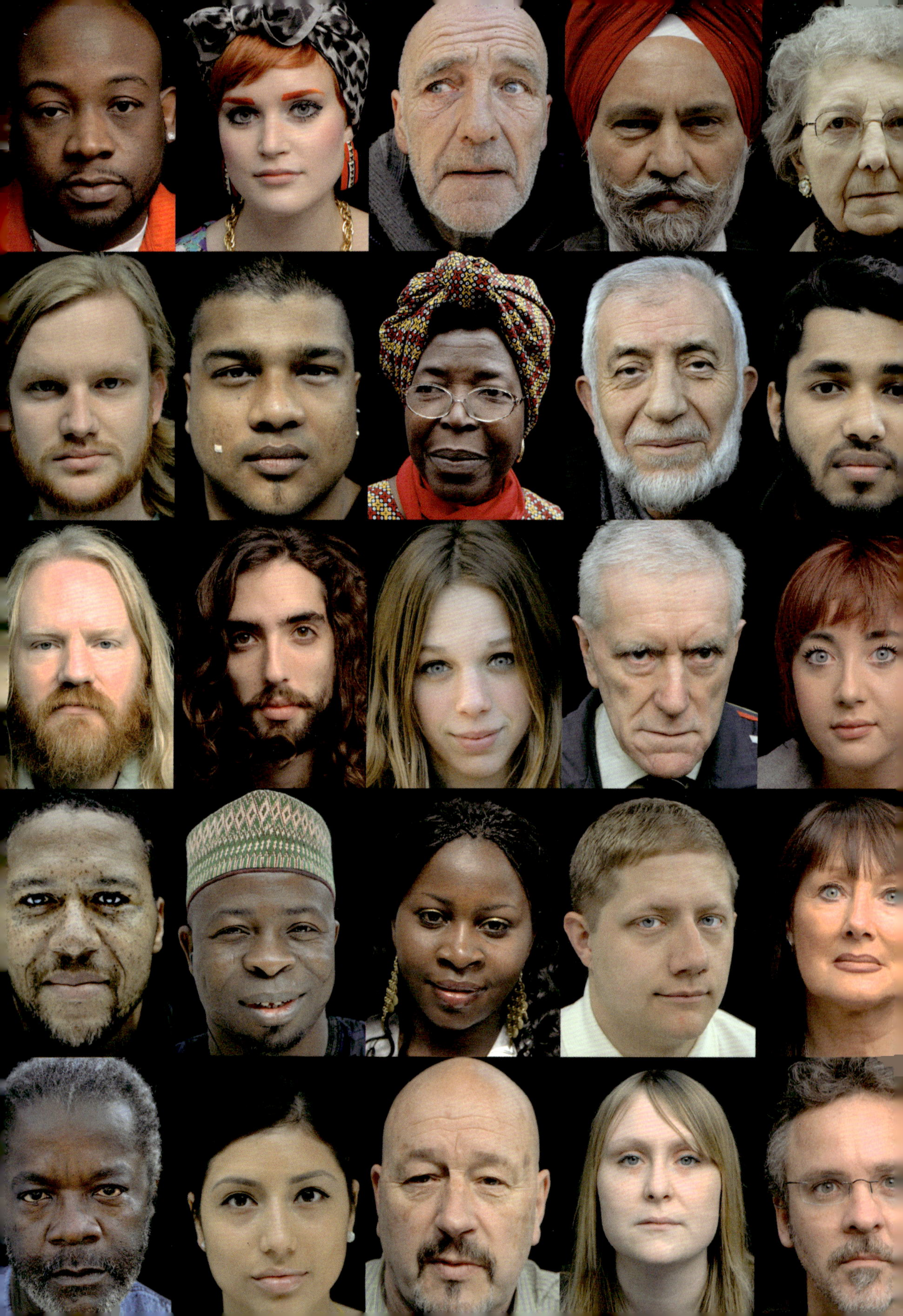

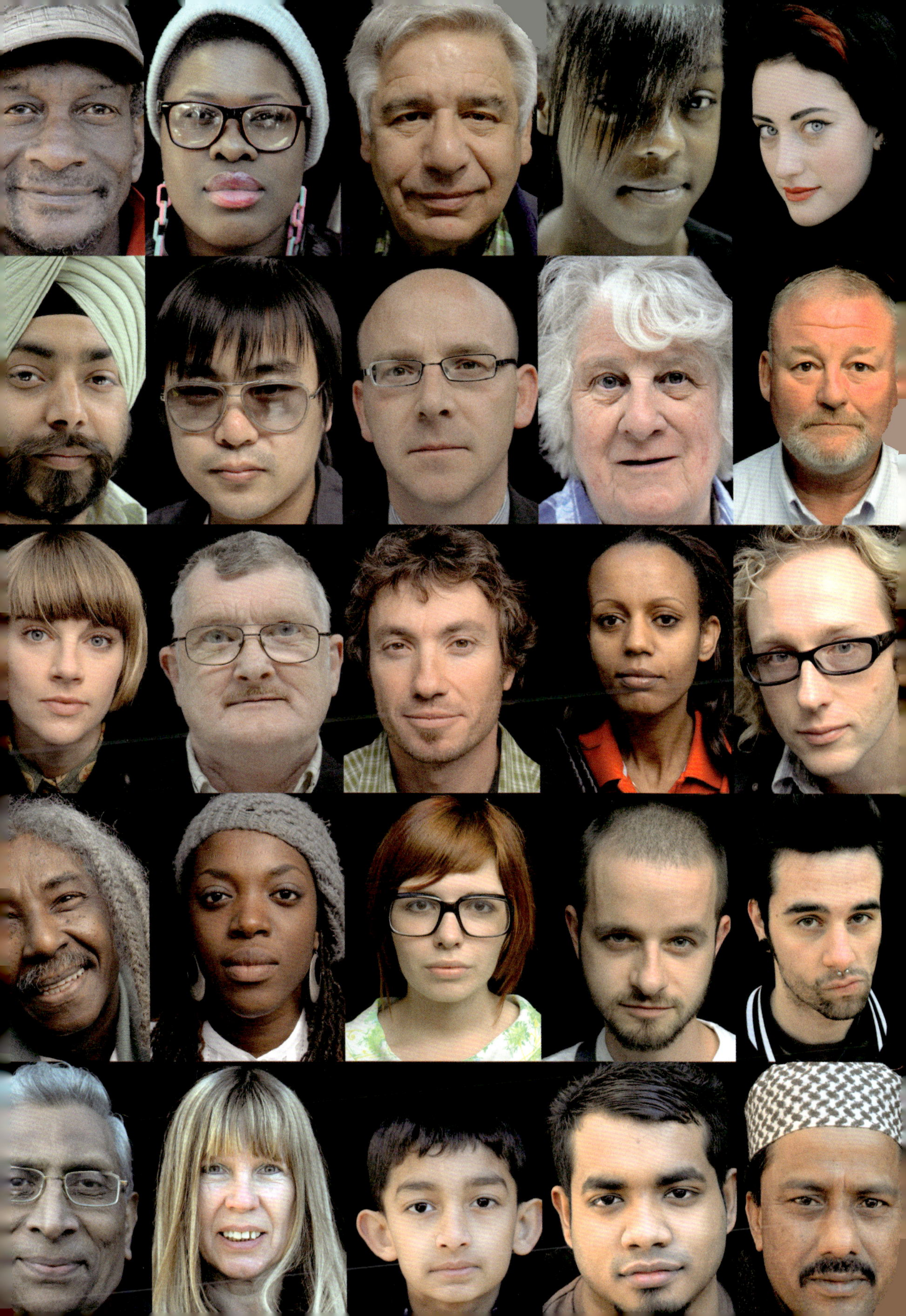

ISLE OF DOGS RE-PHOTOGRAPHY PROJECT

MIKE SEABORNE

In 1983–1986 I undertook an extensive project on the Isle of Dogs to photograph the area prior to its redevelopment. Not only photographing the streets and buildings, but also inside factories, schools and other social spaces. The aim was to document the Island before 'big money' moved in and transformed both the landscape and the people who lived and worked there. The photographs, in both print and digital form, are now part of the Island History Trust archive.

My current project, also being undertaken in partnership with the Island History Trust, is to re-photograph the area and some of the people who remain, now that the redevelopment process is virtually complete, in order to provide a comparative study which will serve both to give the early 1980s photographs a contemporary context, revealing the extent and nature of the changes, and to highlight the significance of the collection as a 'snapshot' of a particularly significant moment in the Island's history.

The re-photography is being done in three ways:

1. Re-photographing scenes, principally streets and buildings, exactly as I photographed them in the early 1980s. This involves finding the precise spot where the original photograph was taken and replicating the view exactly.

2. Re-photographing scenes in a less rigorous way, particularly where the precise spot from which the original photograph was taken cannot now be identified, is inaccessible or simply no longer exists.

3. Re-photographing people, who are obviously now 30 years older, where the original location is no longer applicable or relevant. For example, people I photographed in the 1980s working in factories that subsequently closed, or adults I photographed as children at school.

Top: Westferry Road at its southernmost point, looking east, with the Associated Lead Manufacturing Ltd paint works in the distance, 1985.

Bottom: The same view in 2013 with luxury cars now a more common sight than lorries.

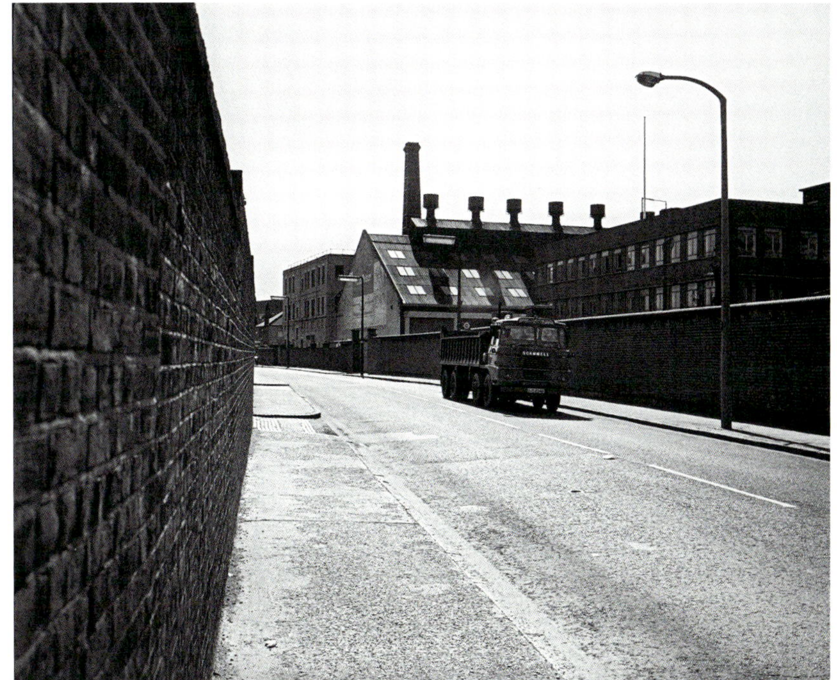

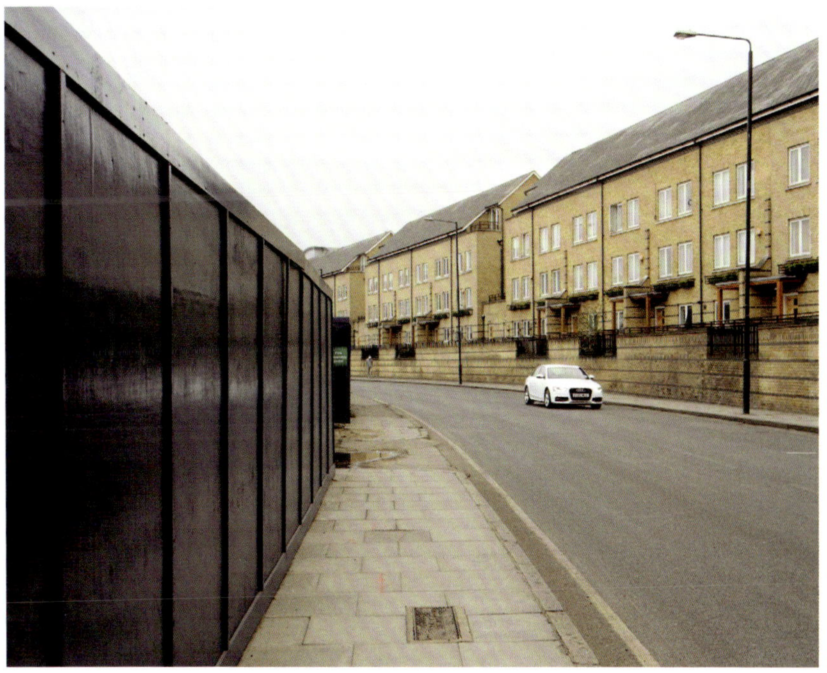

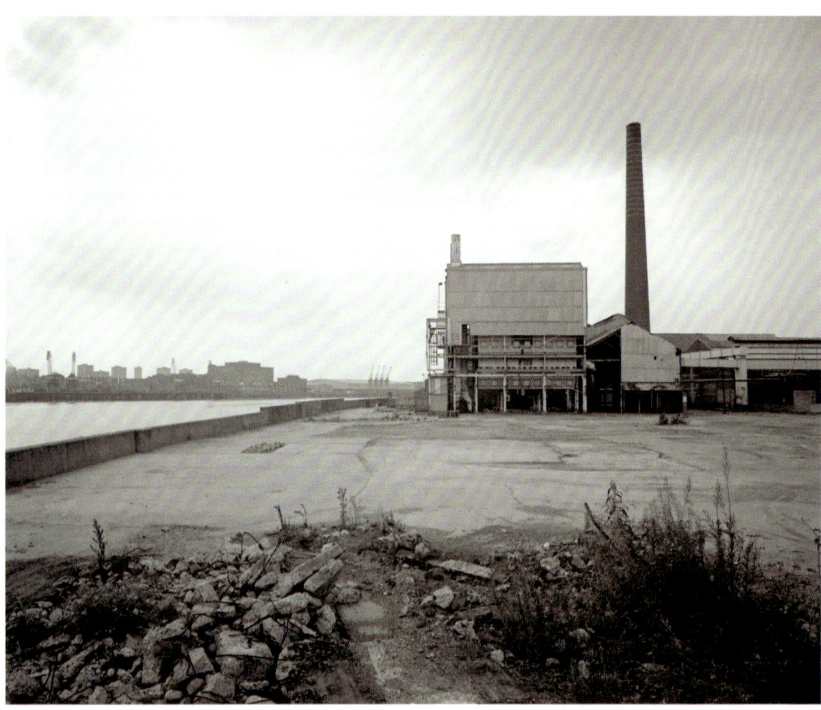

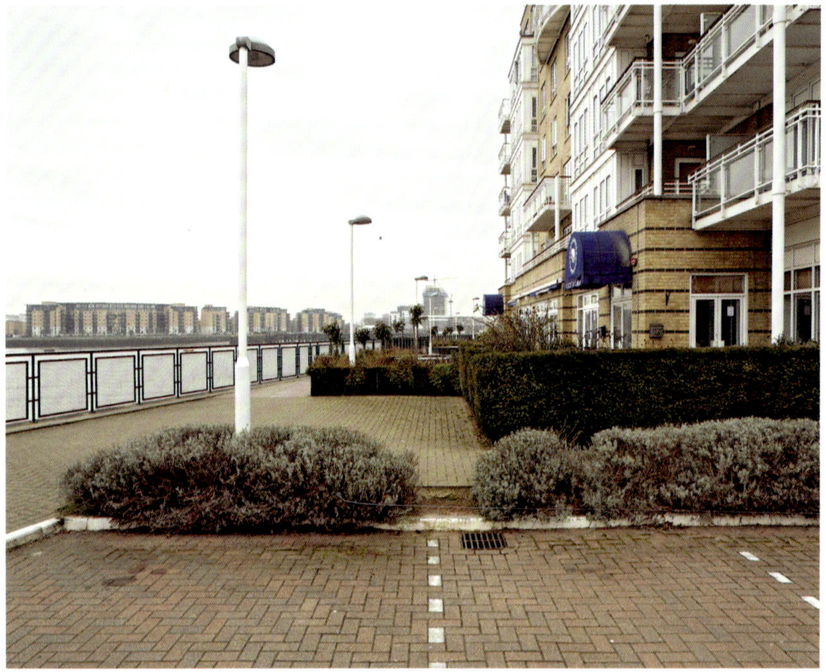

Top: The disused Associated Lead Manufacturing Ltd paint works, Locke's Wharf, Westferry Road, 1986.

Bottom: The same view in 2013 with the site now occupied by riverside apartment blocks.

Top: The Marshal Keate pub (left), Preston's Road looking south, 1983.

Bottom: The same view in 2013. The pub was demolished c. 1987.

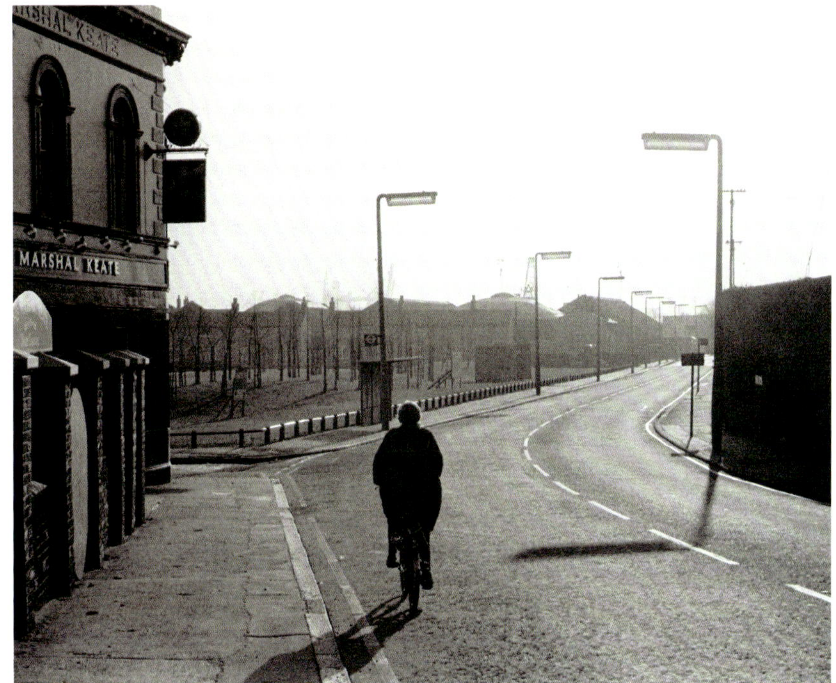

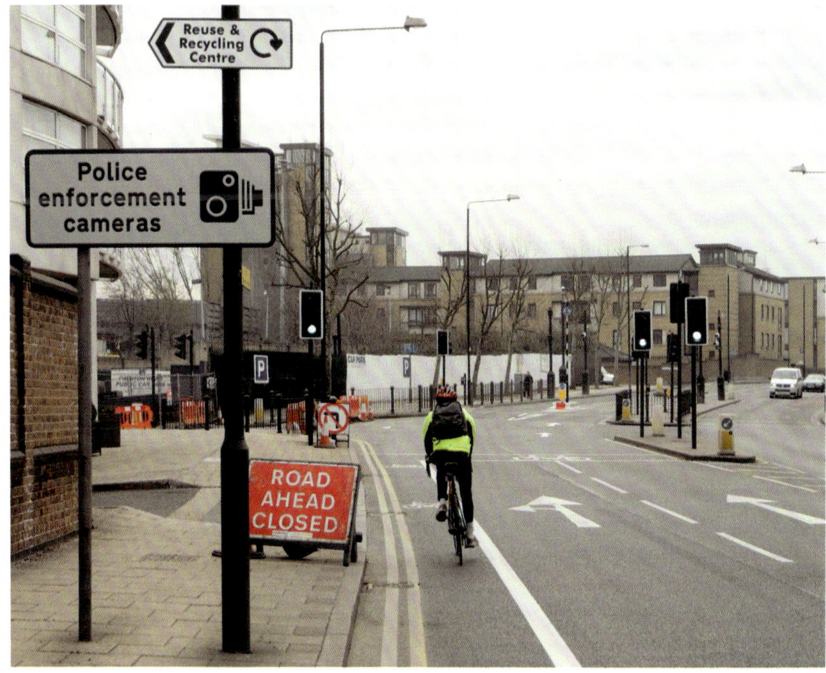

THE HACKNEY FLASHERS

JO SPENCE
WORDS BY SUSAN ANDREWS

One could reasonably argue that all photography is a 'mirror' and a 'window', rather than the either/or dichotomy of practice initially proposed by John Szarkowski in 1960.[1] Recognising the role of the photographer in making any photograph, some practitioners have believed that an individual perspective may obscure or detract from important content and social meaning, so undermining the medium's true purpose as a means of recording. Part of the online digital archive at The Cass contains work from the archive of the photographer, Jo Spence and includes images produced by The Hackney Flashers in the 1970s, of which she was a member. This group adopted an alternative, collective identity rather than one of individualism, viewing the meaning and significance of photography as a social construct, which could be exploited for political ends. The Hackney Flashers placed 'subject matter' at the forefront of their practice with little consideration given to authorship. There was a belief that their photographic vision, based on current feminist ideology, was common to all group members. Whether indeed this was actually the case is difficult to ascertain as a large amount of the work has been lost and much of what remains is hard to credit to a particular individual. However, the common agenda may well have minimised the more obvious individual differences. The group photographed the largely overlooked lives of local women (hence the name 'flashers'), particularly examining places where women worked, the experience of motherhood and childcare. Val Williams notes that "the group's nine women members began to study the use of photography within the capitalist system and to present alternatives. They played a decisive part in establishing a context within which women workers from different cultural fields could work together in pursuit of a collective political aim."[2]

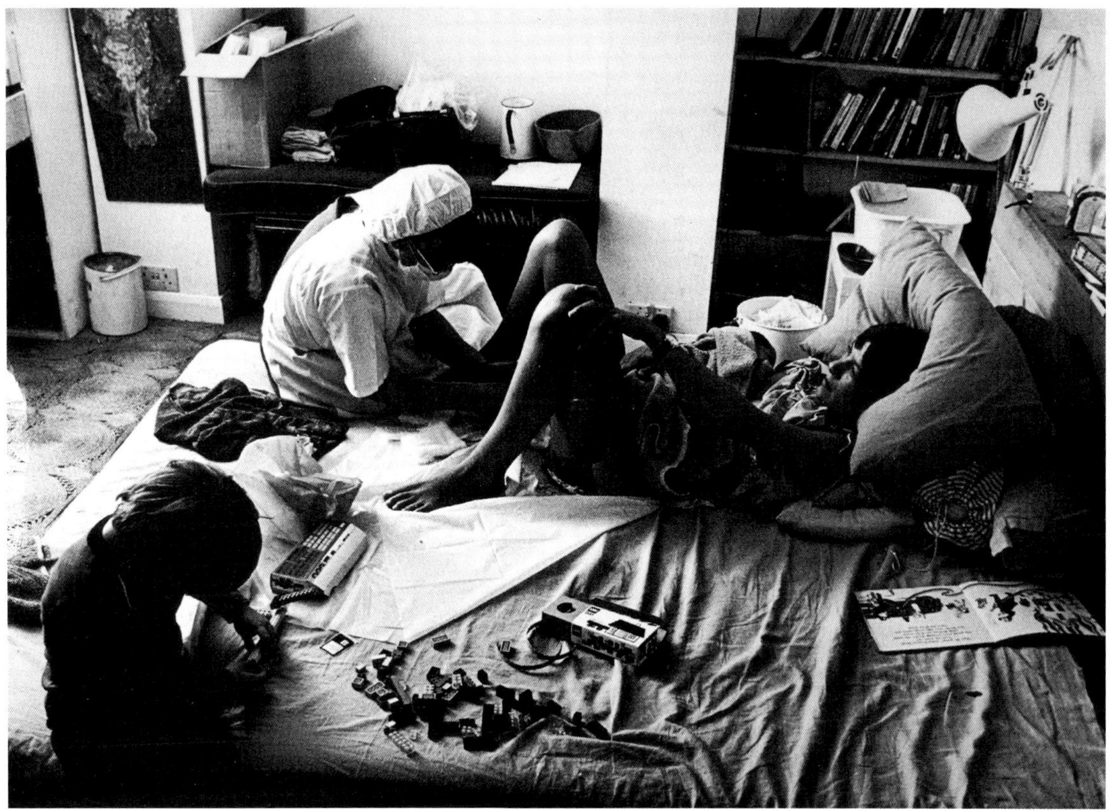

Above and overleaf: Hackney Flashers, from the Jo Spence Archive, Hackney, 1970s.

Challenging received beliefs about documentary photography, the group went on to use cartoons, text and advertisements, which removed the photography from its traditional place and repositioned it as political propaganda, within the tradition of the collages of Heartfield. After the death of Jo Spence what remained of this work was passed to Spence's archivist, Terry Dennett. Dennett is disappointed that very few critics have actively engaged with this type of work (this may be partly due to its collective nature in a culture that reveres celebrity) but identifies the importance of the project as "the only long term all women's project of its kind to emerge in the UK. Carried out on behalf of the Hackney Trades Council with the support of the Labour Hackney Council, the collective was given access to factories, hospitals, libraries and public buildings and even a police station (something not possible today). The work took place just as the old Hackney with its sweatshops and working class inhabitants were being moved out—it is a rare documentation of the end of an era."[3]

Viewed as individual images, appreciation of the work would be limited but seen as a 'body of work' one can understand how the experimental, political and feminist agenda, the working practice and photographic techniques, shaped the work and reflected ideologies.

1. Szarkowski, John, *Mirrors and Windows—American Photography since 1960*, New York: Museum of Modern Art, 1978
2. Williams, Val, *The Other Observers*, London: Virago Press, 1986, p. 172.
3. Interview with Terry Dennett, June, 2013.

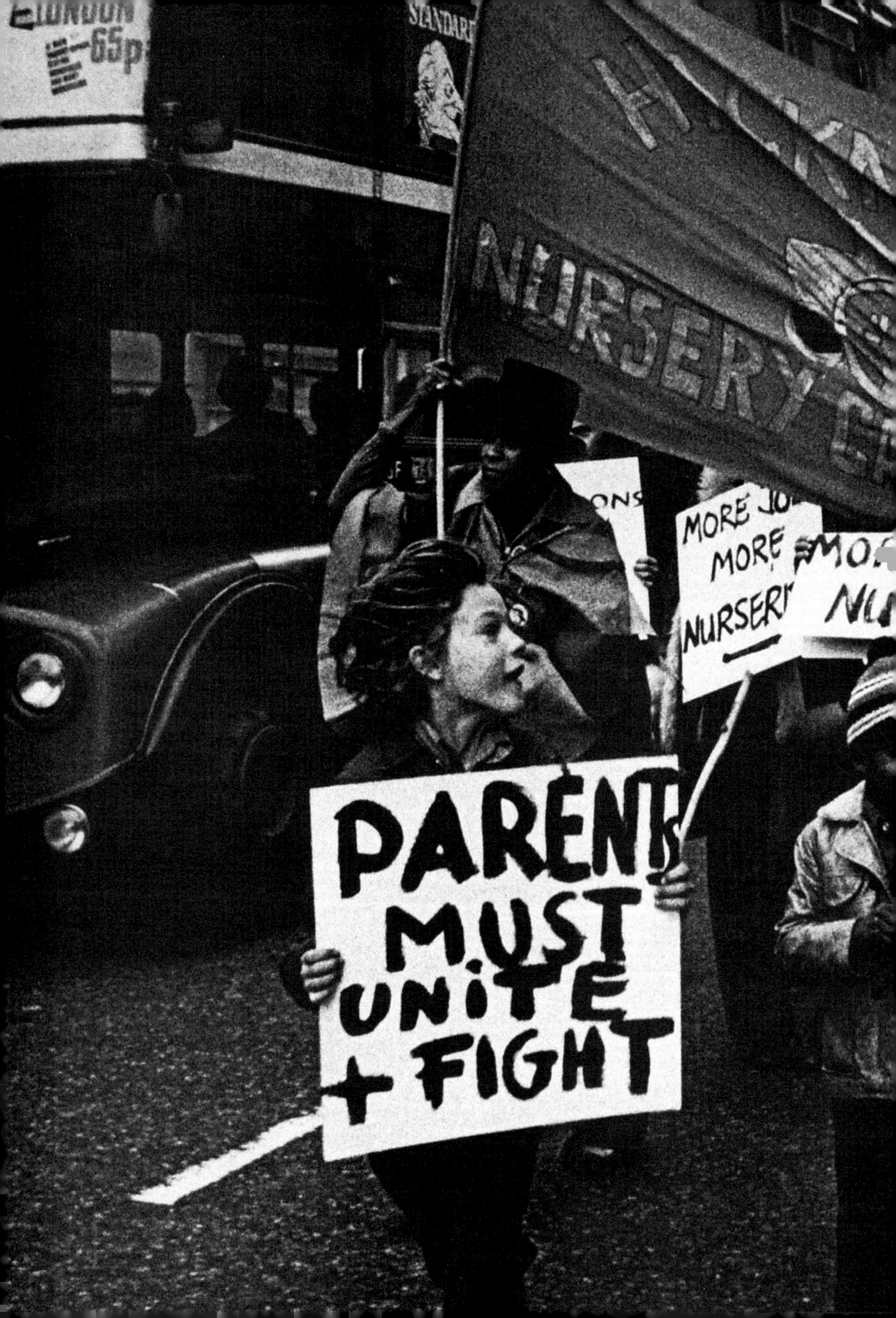

PARENTS
MUST
UNITE
+ FIGHT

NURSERY

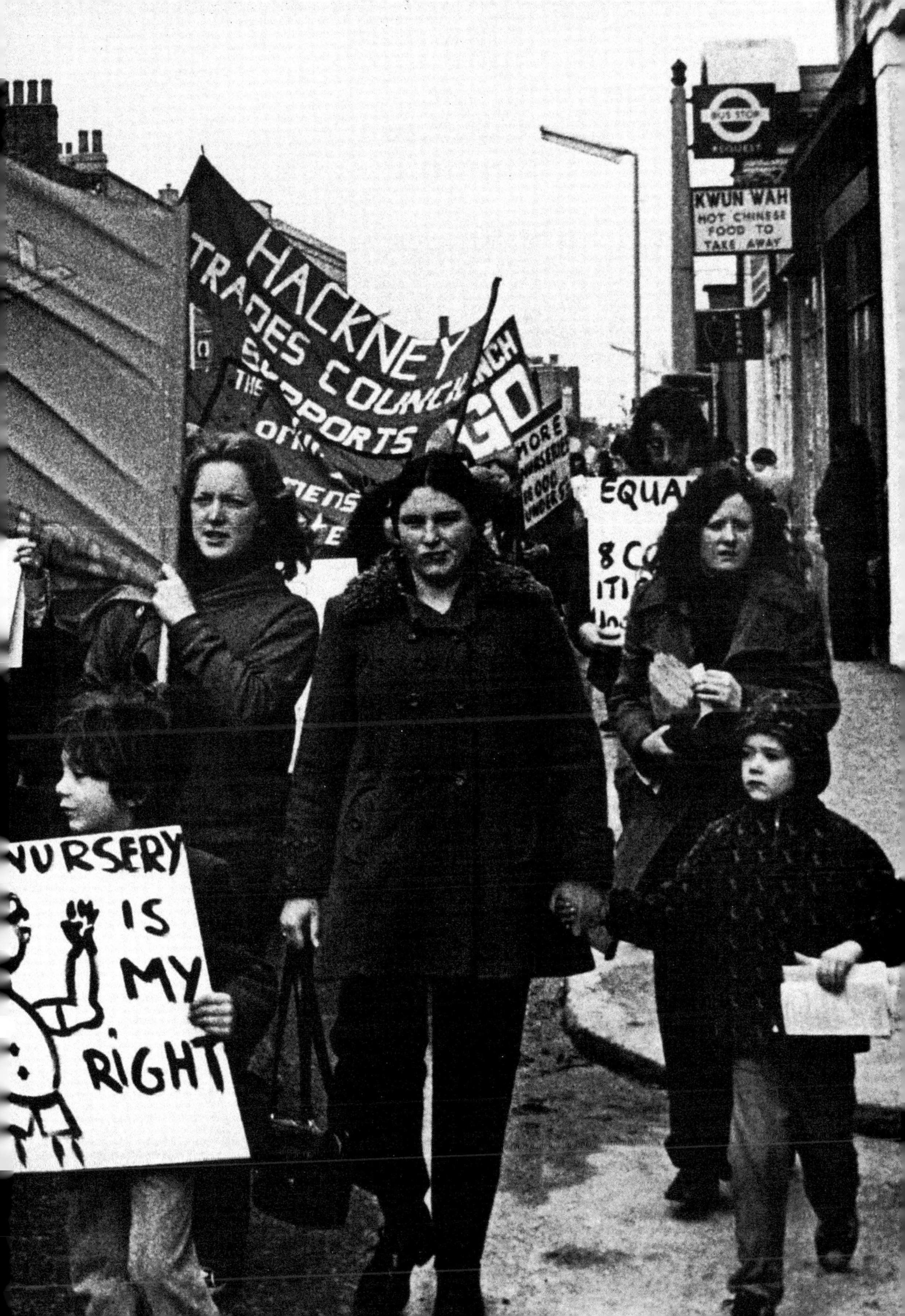
HACKNEY
TRADES COUNCIL
KWUN WAH
HOT CHINESE
FOOD TO
TAKE AWAY
BUS STOP
NURSERY
IS
MY
RIGHT
MORE

THE PHOTO-DIARIES OF MICK WILLIAMSON
WORDS BY SUSAN ANDREWS

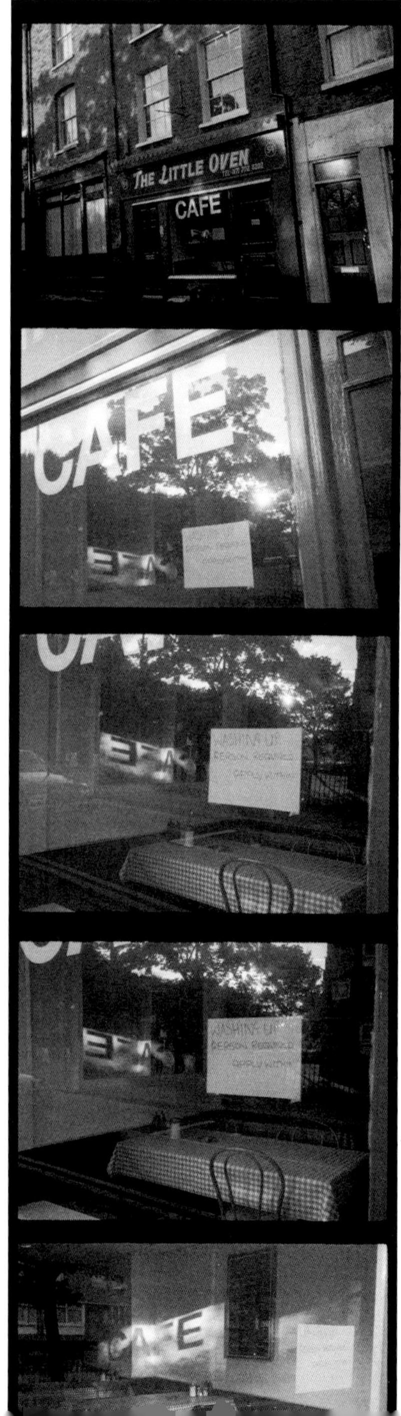

Mick Williamson turns his attention to the everyday; he is never without his Olympus half-frame camera, which accompanies him everywhere. Over the years Williamson's camera has almost become an extension of his body and he appears to sense or feel the photographs (rarely looking through the viewfinder) so in tune is he with this small machine. This working method means that his subject matter often exists on the margins both literally and symbolically where ordinary, routine and frequently domestic events are snatched from the periphery of vision and brought back to the viewer's attention through the act of photography.

Williamson's method of working appears reminiscent of one espoused in Eugene Herrigel's, *Zen in the Art of Archery*, upon which Cartier-Bresson based his photographic ethos.[1] Herrigel's close analysis of the training by the master of *Kyudo* (the Japanese Art of the bow) and particularly that of *Daishadokyo*, which places great emphasis on the spiritual aspect, means that the archer is so adapted and skilled that his practice becomes mentally and physically effortless. In the foreword to this book, Daisetz T Suzuki observes "the archer ceases to be conscious of himself as the one who is engaged in hitting the bull's-eye which confronts him. This state of unconsciousness is realised only when, completely empty and rid of the self, he becomes one with the perfecting of his technical skill, though there is in it something of a quite different order which cannot be attained by any progressive study of the art."[2]

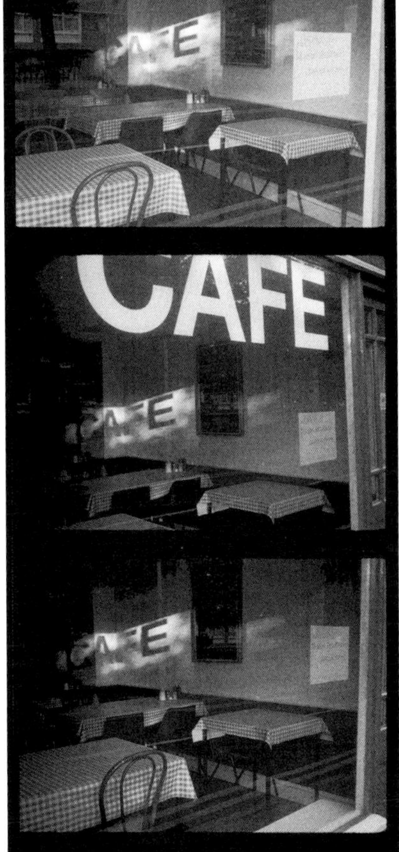

Opposite, above and following pages: Mick Williamson, from the *Photo-Diaries of Mick Williamson*, 1973–2013.

Cartier-Bresson embraced this philosophy in his work: "To me, photography is the simultaneous recognition, in a fraction of a second, of the significance of an event as well as of a precise organisation of forms which give that event its proper expression."[3] This highly influential philosophy is apparent in many of Bresson's photographs where each is formally composed through the viewfinder at the moment of shooting, an approach which came to be known as 'the decisive moment'. Although Mick Williamson's work and method initially seem very different (his images often appear to be stolen from the fringes of vision without formal composition) the photographs, like Bresson's demonstrate a keen awareness of timing and medium. This has been brought about by repeated practice where the artist becomes so habituated with the technology that he sees "intuitively" beyond the medium to the subject. Williamson's knowledge of the fixed lens camera means that he knows without looking what his camera sees, as if his eye has been relocated in his hand. He uses film, which also seems significant as there is still a tiny delay with digital technology and the immediate response of his camera trigger to shutter ensures the moment does not escape. The French title of Bresson's Book, *Images à la Sauvette*, which can loosely be translated as "images on the run" or "stolen images", seems to reflect precisely Williamson's working method: there are never enough seconds in the day and you have to be quick to catch them.[4]

Mick Williamson has carried this camera since the 1970s, when in response to pressure as a professional photographer to make photographs of his family, he bought himself a small amateur camera in order to take pictures like other families. He began by shooting one to two films a week and treating this camera only as a notebook. Over the years this practice has evolved into his *métier* and he is now shooting two to three films a day, gradually building up an immense body of work. Williamson doesn't know how many images the archive contains, but there must be well over a million, which of course raises the question, how does one deal with this volume of work and how might the images be seen? In many ways the work begins after the shooting, processing and darkroom contact sheets, when the editing and selection is done.

The East End Archive has put together an initial selection from "The Photo-Diaries of Mick Williamson" that relates to The Cass and E1 area where he works. However, the archive team is still considering the collection, as there is so much to choose from and each choice would create different inflections of the practice. Recently, Williamson has selected images on the basis of sequences, groups of images shot consecutively, which reflect his interest in movement and change, but this is not how they are always seen; sometimes they are projections or large scale images and sometimes tiny prints, presented floating in small frames. However, what many of these photographs have in common, at least those that have been selected, is a strong sense of the transformative nature of light, making the ordinary, extraordinary. Whilst most of the shooting takes place within a busy everyday schedule, the photographs offer an opportunity for stillness and evaluation and indeed there is often a meditative quality to the work where the intense quality of light surpasses the photographed subject, converting it into a metaphor. The snatched, seemingly irrelevant manner of taking the photographs belies the fact that the printed images appear as small revelations.

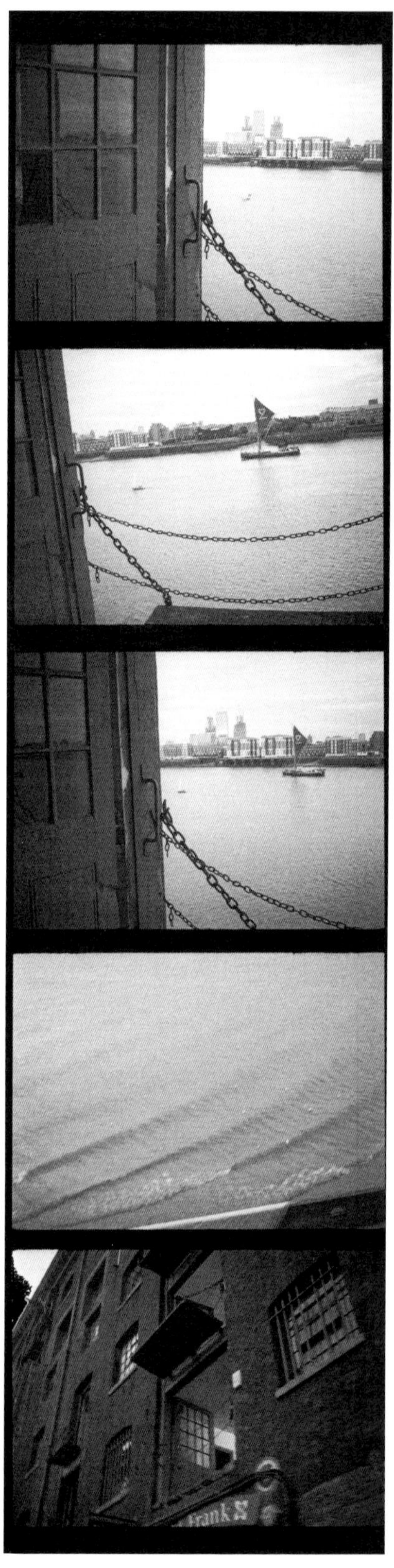

What is the motivation behind such an obsessive practice? Williamson's work is definitely not heroic photography, which hunts for the 'exotic other', once the mark of documentary photographers and photojournalists. His is a quiet approach, both in its taking and its making. The photographs certainly describe the life of a man as he commutes to work, enjoys his family, friends and travel. In as much he may be seen as a social documentarian, and perhaps these images represent an affirmation of his existence. Essentially, he is a collector of memories, of lost moments and of the ephemeral, which may be what draws him to the light, itself in constant motion, effecting continuous change, something intangible now trapped in silver gelatin. This action of light upon the object reminds us that the ordinary is wonderful. Maybe these images are a reflection of desire and the self-portrait of an unassuming man as he recognises the potential of the world.

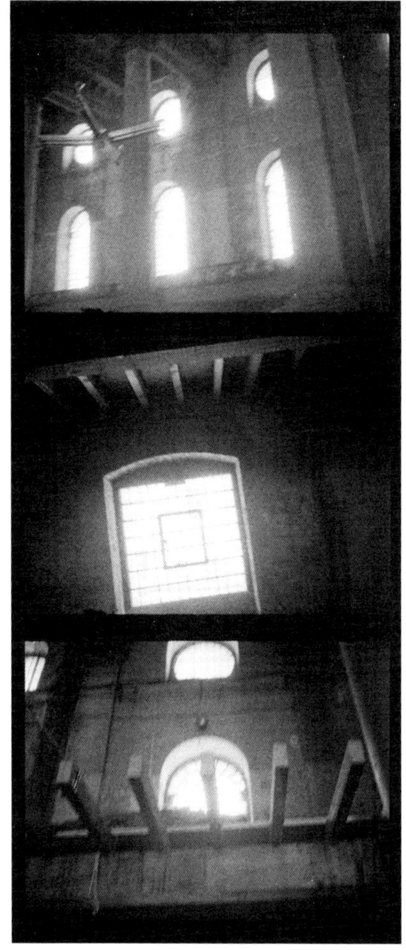

1. Herrigel, Eugene, *Zen in the Art of Archery*, London: Routledge and Kegan Paul, 1953.

2. Herrigel, Eugene, *Zen in the Art of Archery*, London: Penguin Books, 2004, p. 6.

3. Cartier-Bresson, Henri, "The Decisive Moment", in Peter Pollack, ed., *The Picture History of Photography: From the earliest beginnings to the present day*, London: Thames and Hudson, 1977, p. 155.

4. Cartier-Bresson, Henri, *Images à la Sauvette*, Paris: Editions Verve, 1952. Cartier-Bresson, Henri, *The Decisive Moment*, New York: Simon and Schuster, 1952.

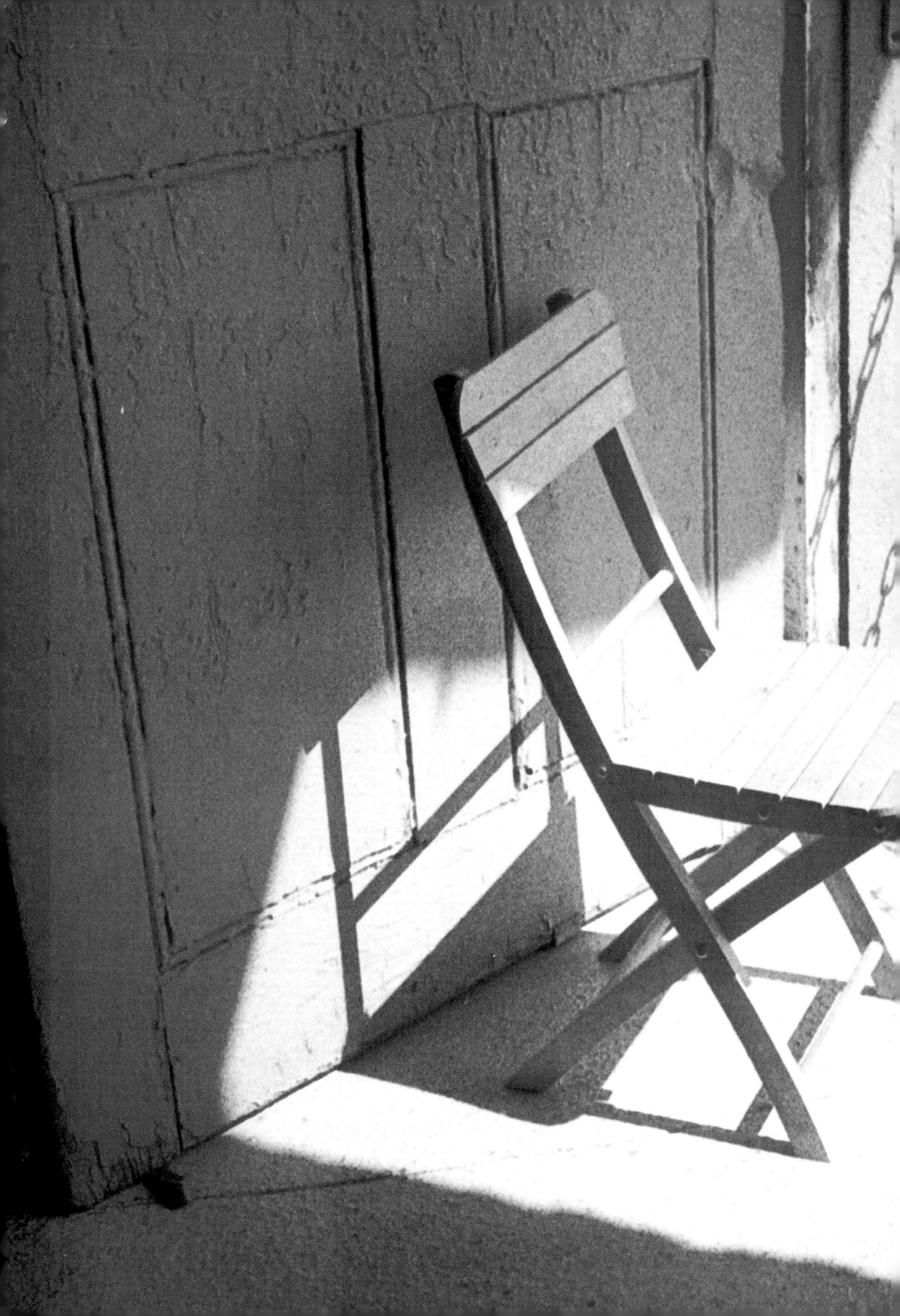

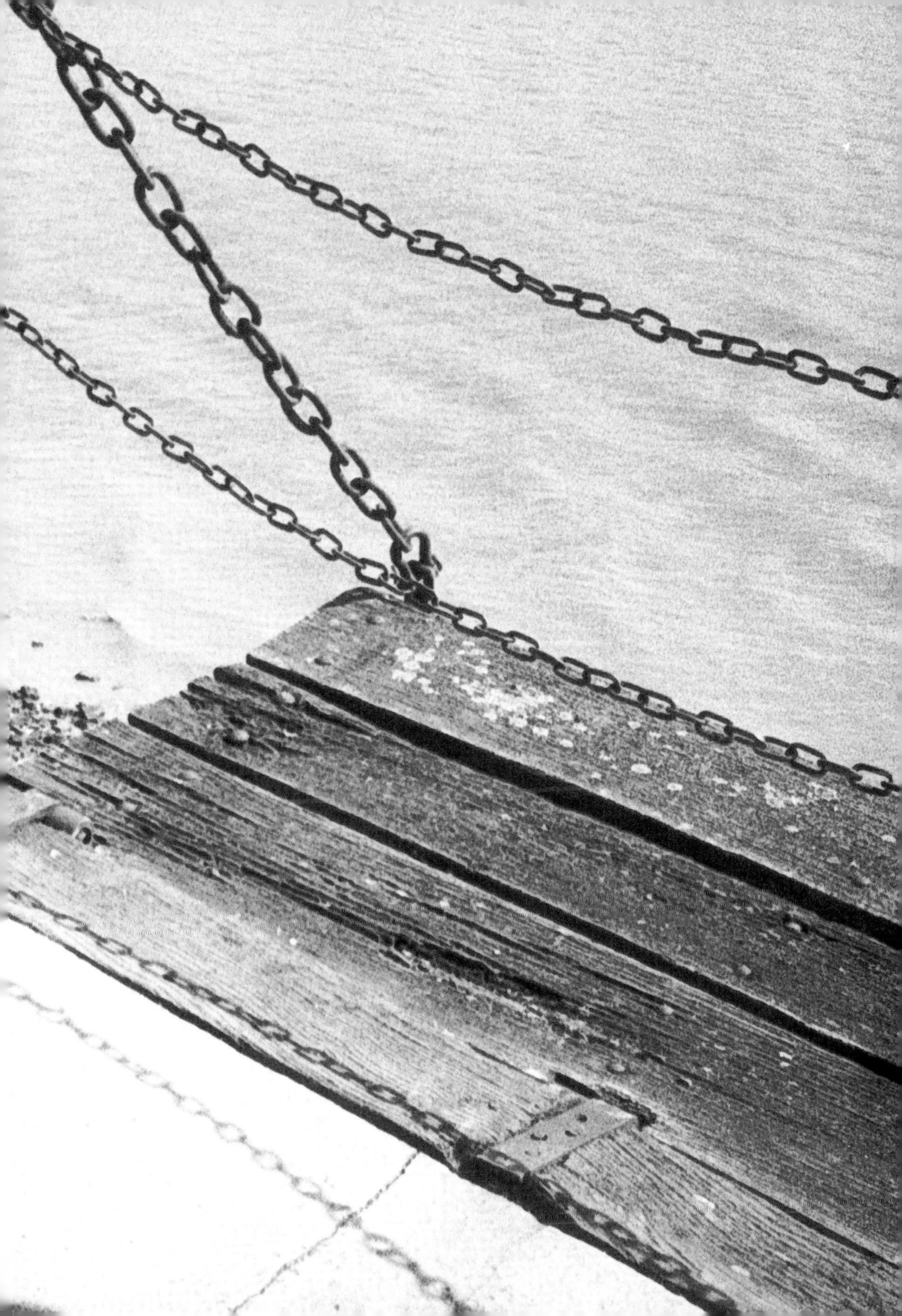

LIST OF ILLUSTRATIONS

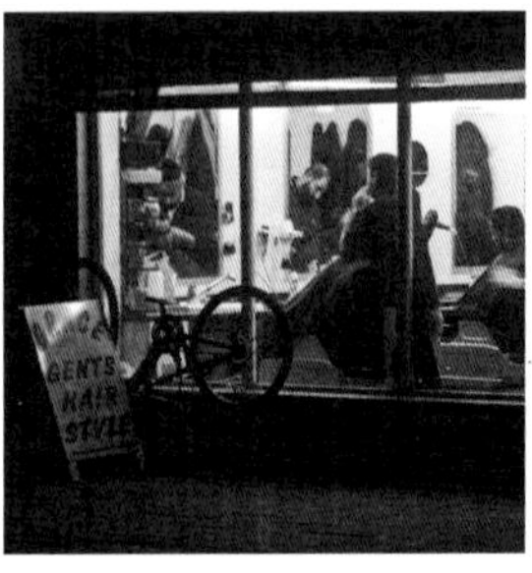

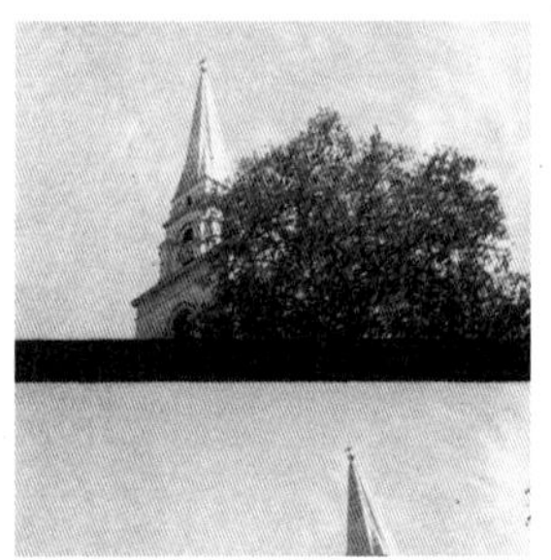

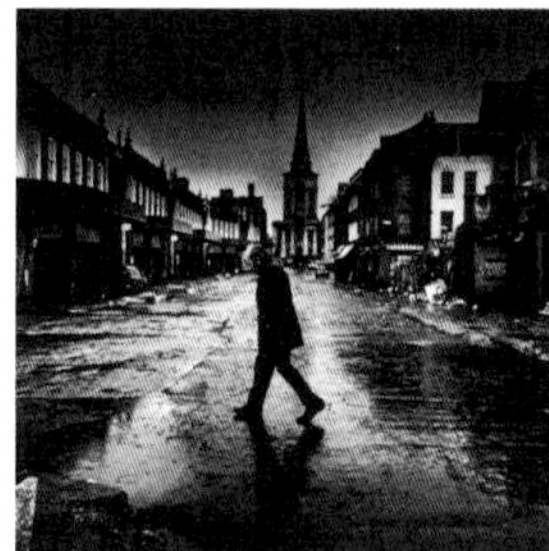

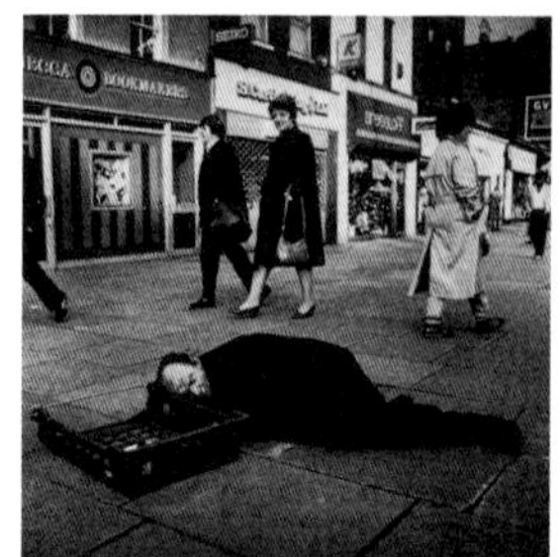

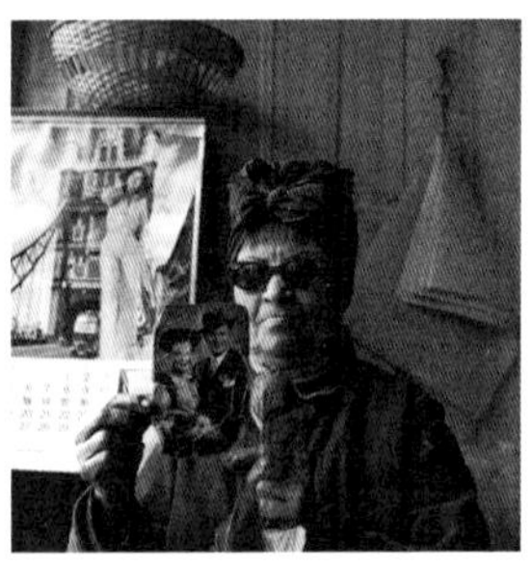

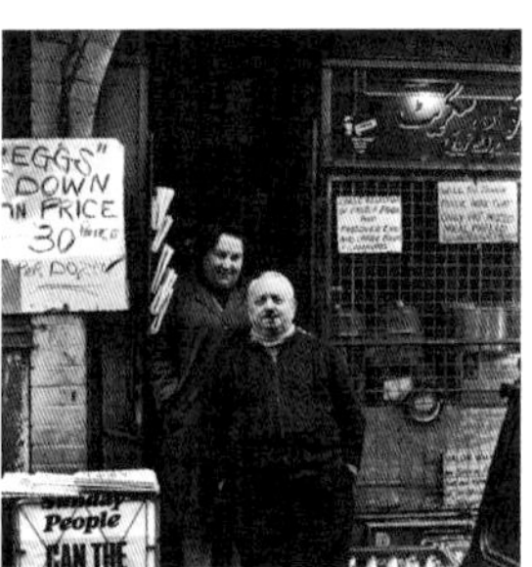

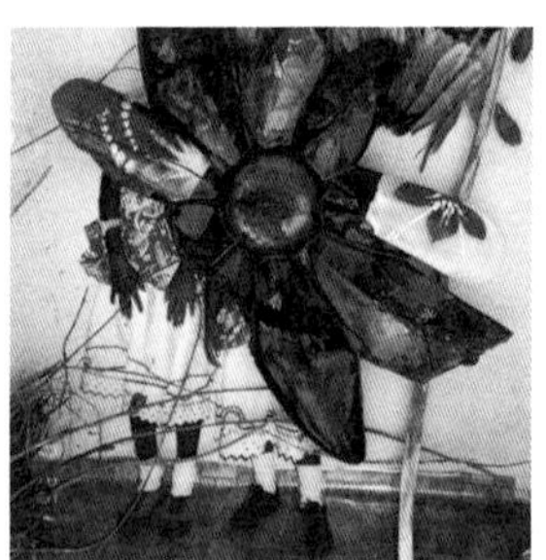

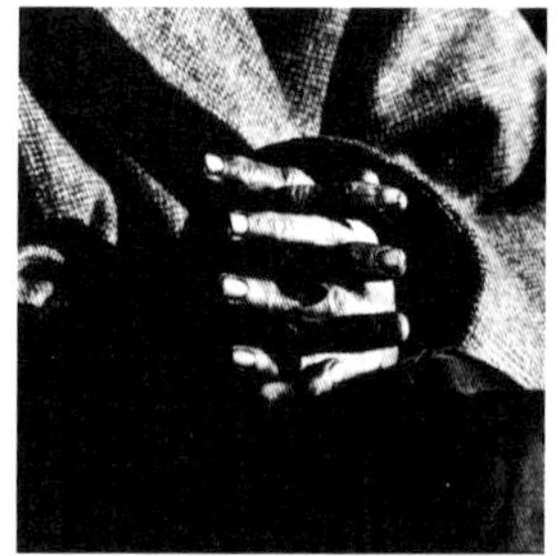

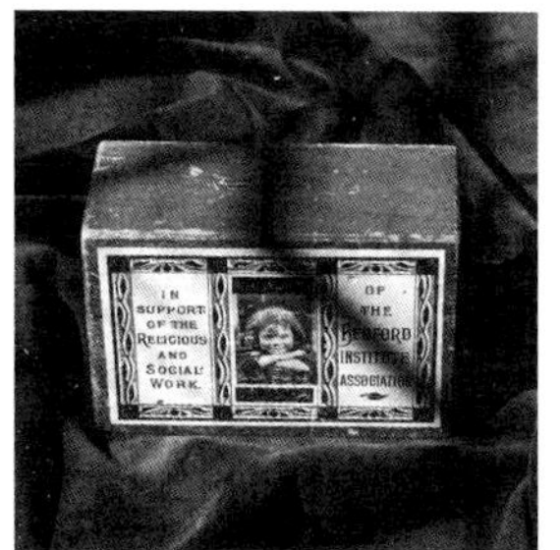

p. 16
Nicholas Haeffner, Donation Box with photo by Horace Warner, 2013. Courtesy of Hoxton Hall Archive.

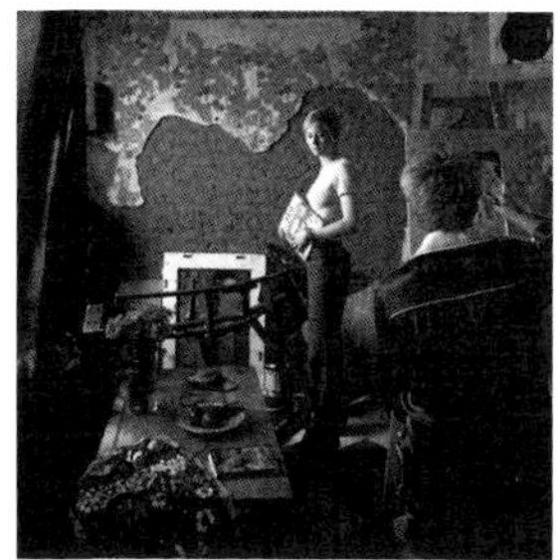

p. 19
Tom Hunter, *The Art of Squatting*, Hackney, 1997.

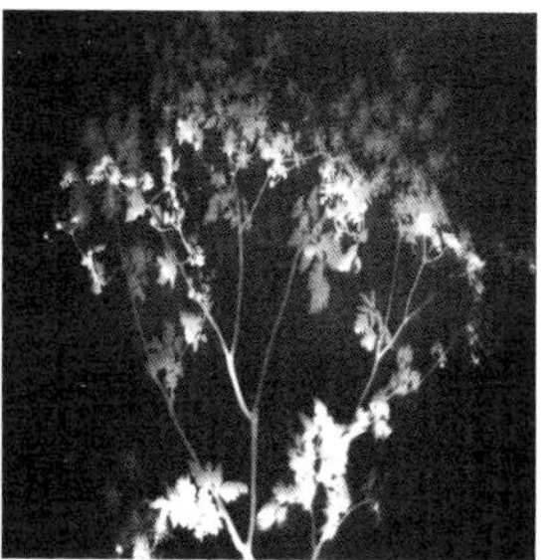

p. 21
Susan Andrews, *After Anna Atkins, Anthriscus sylvestris (cow parsley)* cyanotype, 2010.

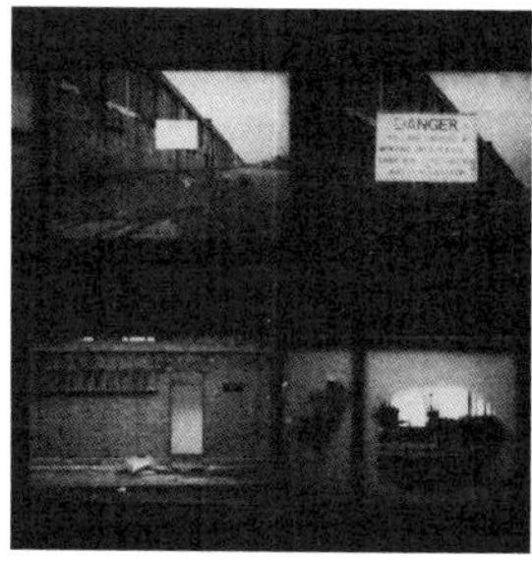

p. 22
Susan Andrews, Royal Albert Docks (now London City Airport), c. 1980.

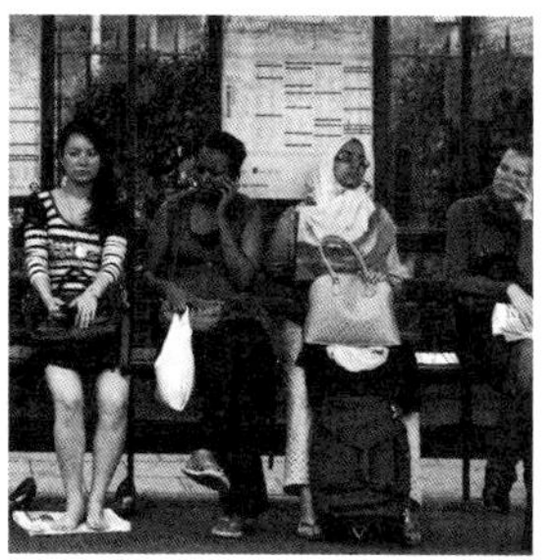

pp. 25–29
Susan Andrews, from the series *Up and Down Whitechapel High Street (A11)*, 2009–2013.

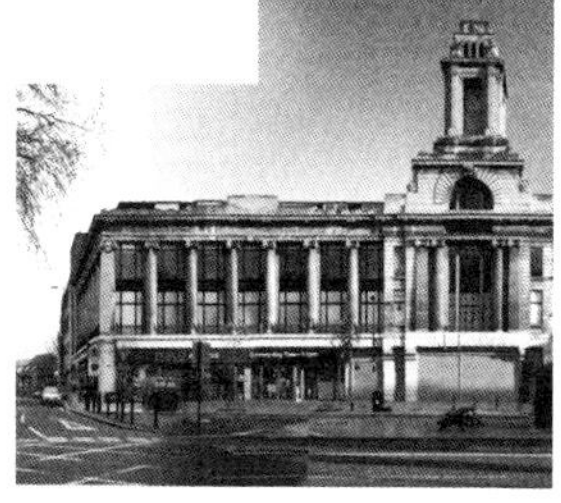

pp. 30–31
The Building Exploratory, *Panorama High Street East 2012*, Whitechapel High Street, 2012. Thanks to the Building Exploratory. The project can be viewed at: www.panoramaeast.org.uk.

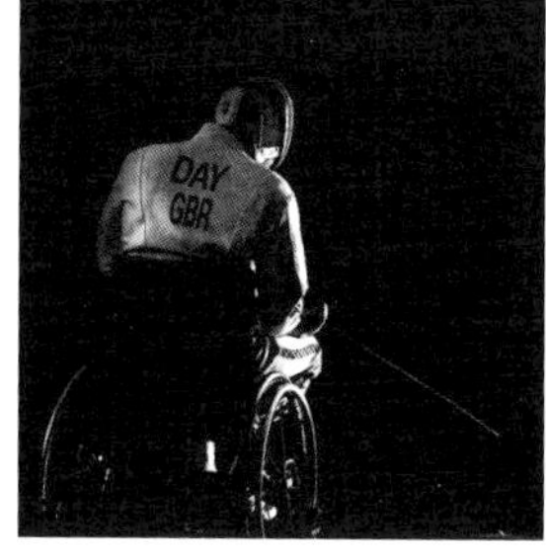

p. 35
Ian Farrant, *Ian Day, wheelchair fencing*, 2011. Extract from a conversation with Michael Upton. Full text online at www.eastendarchive.org.

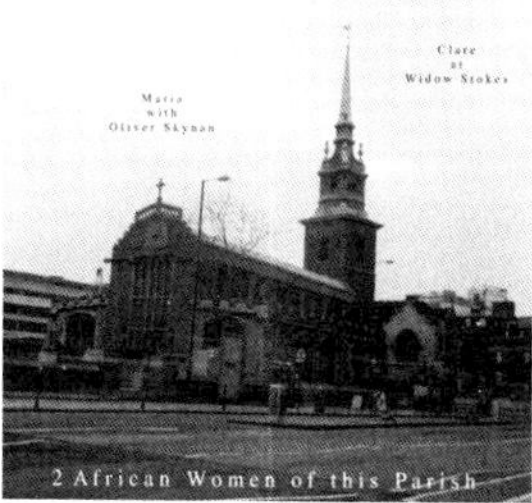

p. 38
Joy Gregory, All Hallows, from the series *Sites of Africa*, c. 1990. Originally published in *Critical Cities: Ideas, Knowledge and Agitation, vol. 2*, ed. Deepa Naik and Trenton Oldfield, Myrdle Court Press: London, 2010.

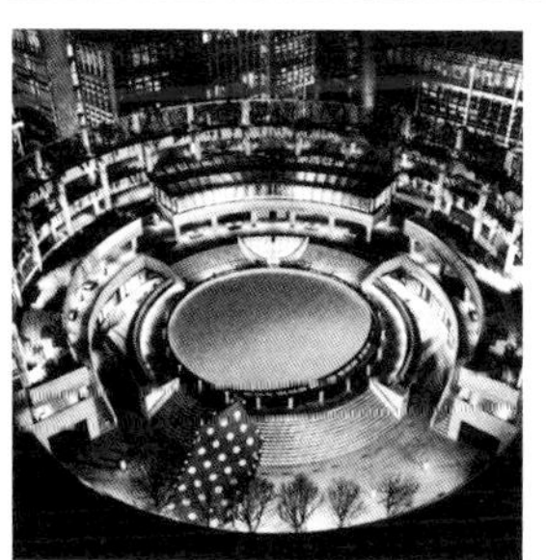

p. 43
Brian Griffin, *Big Tie*, from the *Broadgate Project*, 1987.

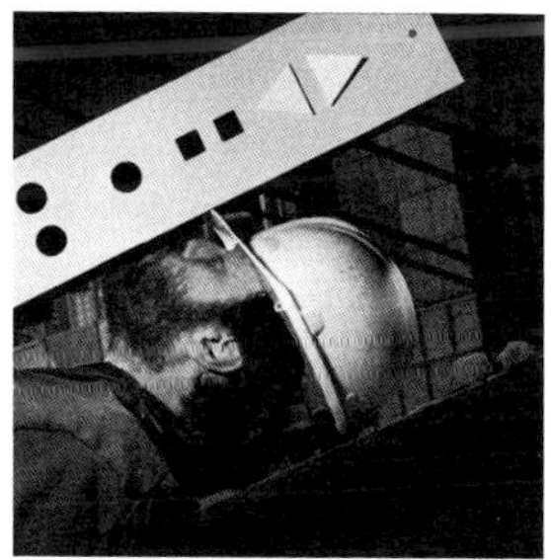

pp. 44–45
Brian Griffin, Carpenter, Lift Engineer, Plasterer, Sewage Pipe Layer, from the *Broadgate Project*, 1986. Commissioned by Rosehaugh Stanhope.

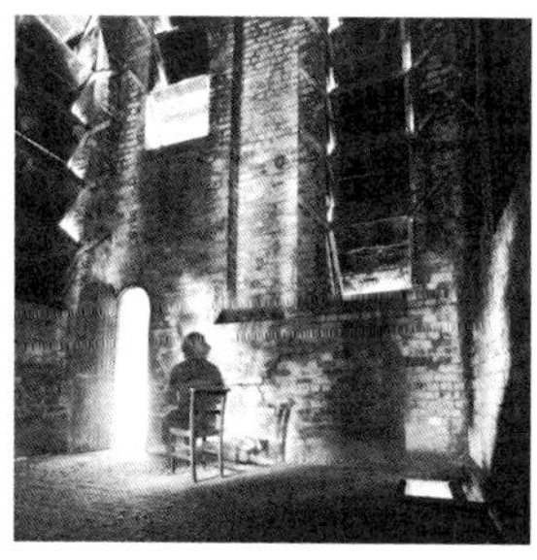

p. 47
Spencer Rowell, St Ignatius Church, Stamford Hill, 2011.

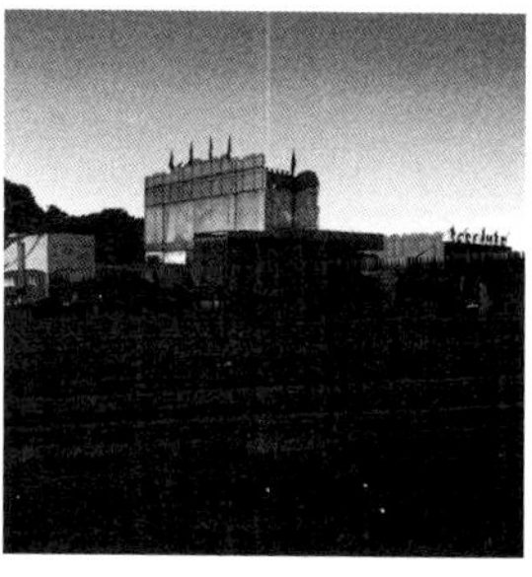

p. 48
David George, Leytonstone High Street, 2011.

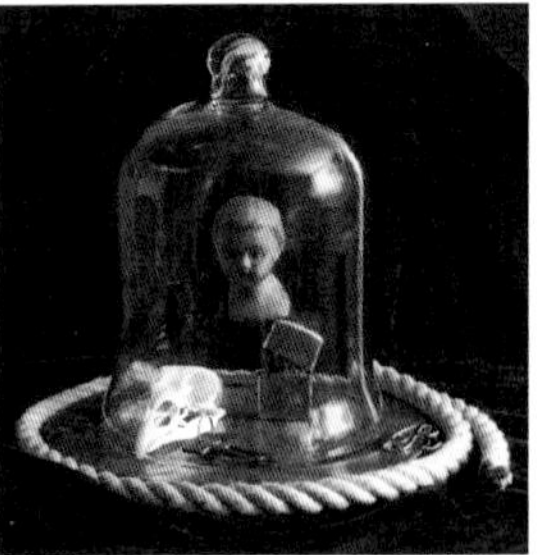

p. 51
Nicholas Haeffner, *Hysterical Symptoms: Objects of Threat and Betrayal*, 2013.

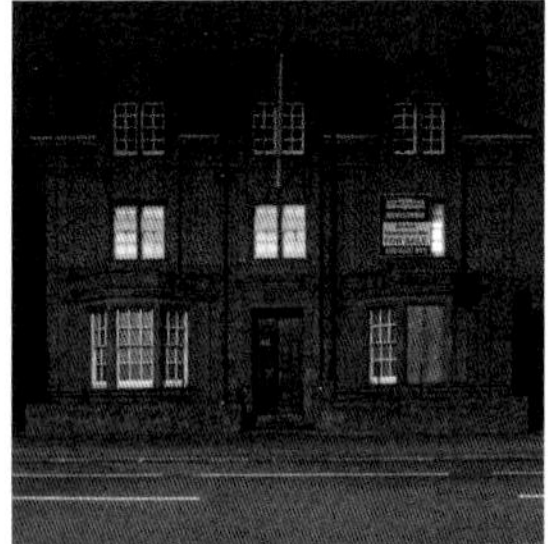

p. 52
David George, Police Station, Leytonstone High Street, 2011.

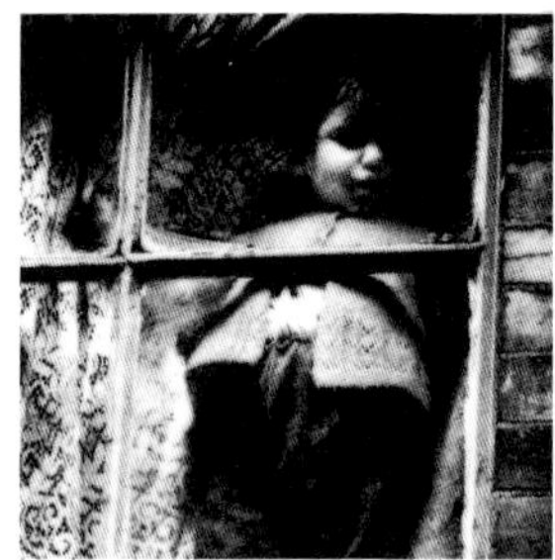

p. 52
John Claridge, *Child at window, E2, 1962.* "There is always one moment in childhood when the door opens and lets the future in", Graham Greene.

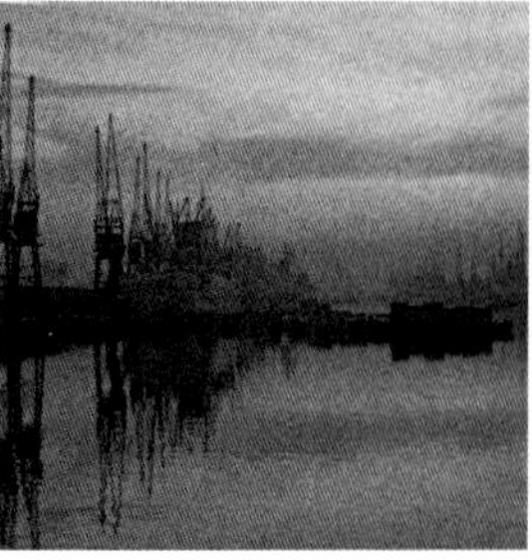

p. 53
John Claridge, London Docks, E16, 1964. "Every night I used to go to sleep hearing the sound of the docks, and in my dreams off to unknown lands", John Claridge.

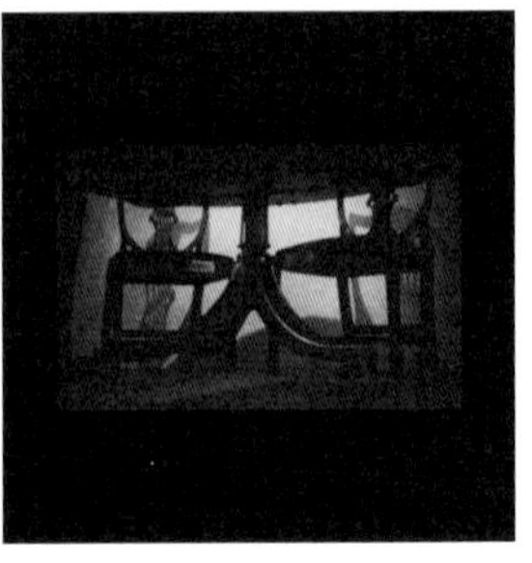

p. 54
Spencer Rowell, 2011.

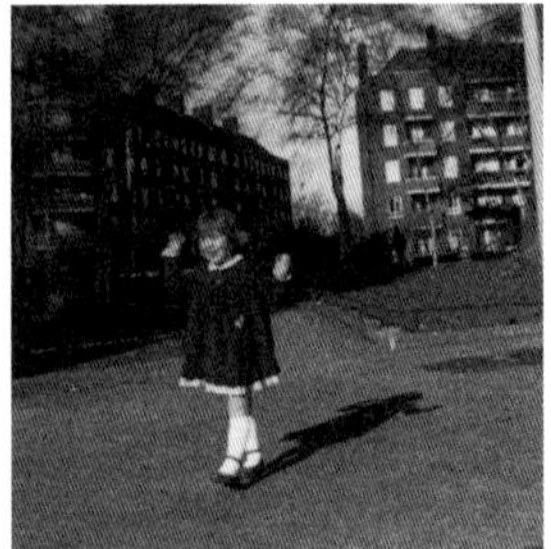

pp. 56–61
Images from family albums belonging to the residents of Woodberry Down. Text edited from a conversation with Michael Upton, full version available at www.eastendarchive.org.uk.

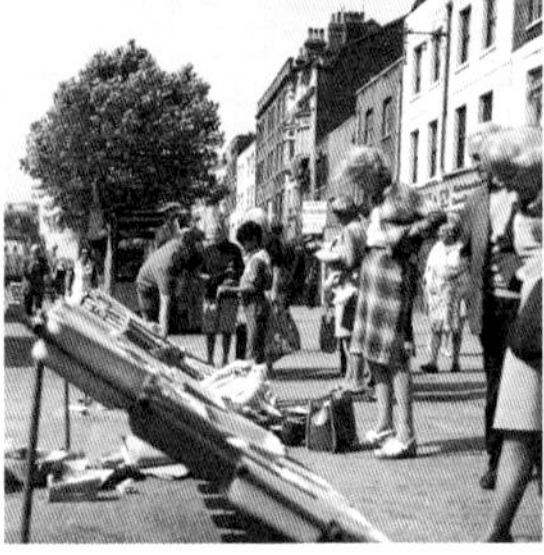

p. 63
Found image, Whitechapel High Street, c. 1971. Don Shewan/Steve Pratt/Brian Canarens, commissioned by the Geography Department, Queen Mary College.

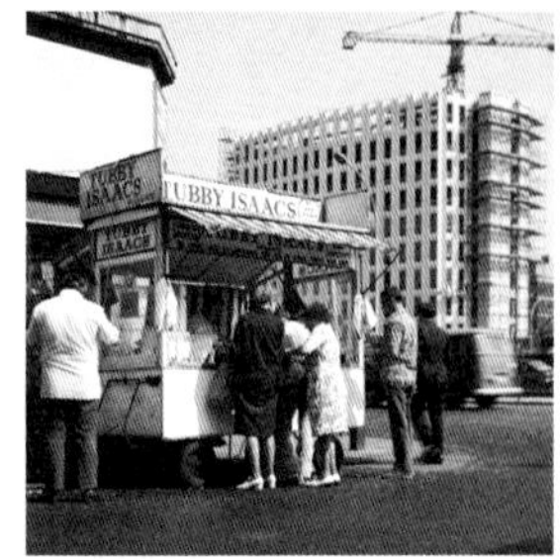

p. 65
Found image, Goulston Street, c. 1972. Don Shewan/Steve Pratt/Brian Canarens, commissioned by the Geography Department, Queen Mary College.

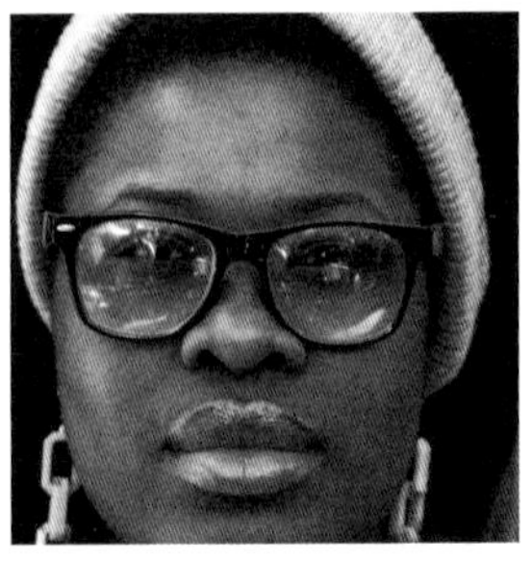

pp. 73–75
Heather McDonough and Rod Morris, from the series *Recognition*, 2011. Project commissioned by the Museum of London and the Hackney Museum, 2011.

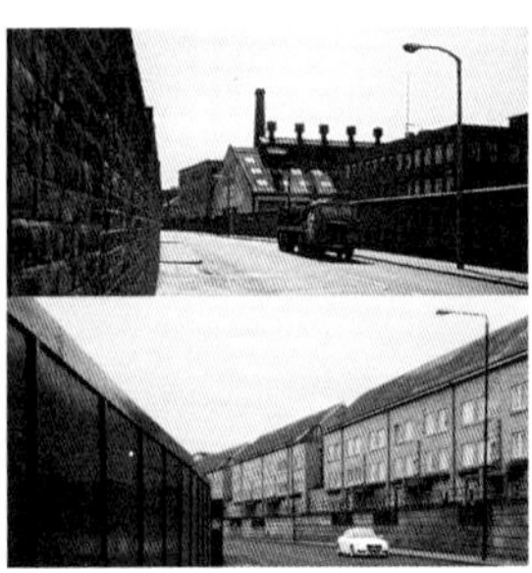

pp. 77–79
Mike Seaborne, Isle of Dogs, from the *Isle of Dogs Re-photography project*, 1983–6 and 2013.

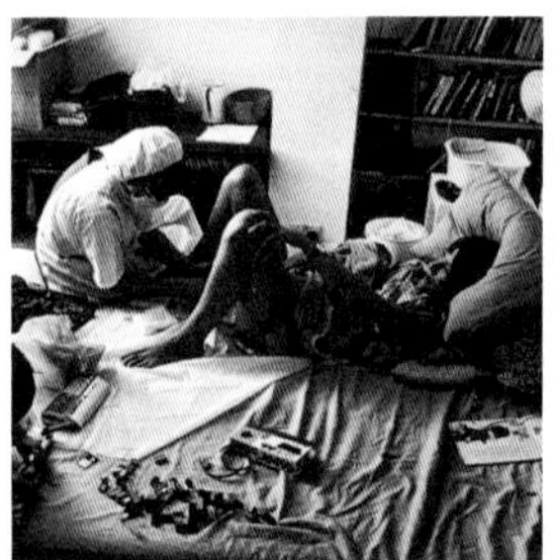

p. 81
Hackney Flashers, from the Jo Spence Archive, Hackney, 1970s. From the Jo Spence Archive, thanks to Terry Dennett.

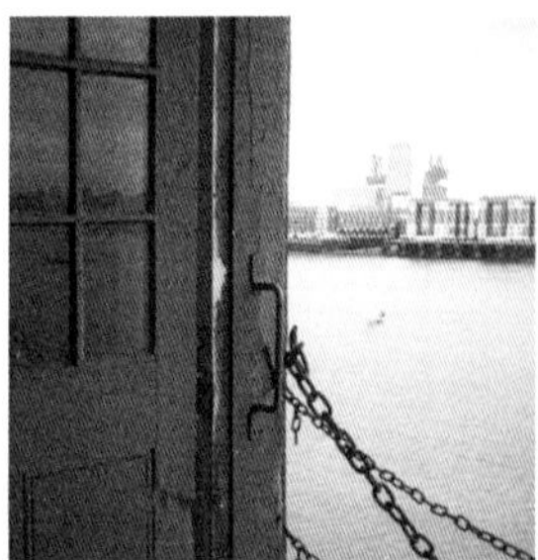

pp. 84–89
Mick Williamson, from the *Photo-Diaries of Mick Williamson*, 1973–2013.

CONTACTS

Susan Andrews
www.susanandrews.co.uk

Stephen Berkoff
gallery@lucy-bell.com

Building Exploratory
panoramaeast.org.uk

John Claridge
www.johnclaridge
photographer.com

Ian Farrant
www.ianfarrant.co.uk

David George
www.davidgeorge.eu

Joy Gregory
www.joygregory.co.uk

Brian Griffin
www.briangriffin.co.uk

Nicholas Haeffner
www.nickhaeffner.co.uk

David Howells
davidrichardhowells
@googlemail.com

Tom Hunter
www.tomhunter.org

Don McCullin
www.facebook.com/
DonMcCullinPhotography

Heather McDonough
www.heathermcdonough.com

Rod Morris
www.rodmorris.co.uk

Spencer Rowell
www.spencerrowell.co.uk

Mike Seaborne
www.mikeseaborne.com

Jo Spence
(contact Terry Dennett)
www.jospence.org

Michael Upton
m.upton@londonmet.ac.uk

Mick Williamson
www.mickwilliamson.com

AUTHORS

Susan Andrews
Susan Andrews is Reader in Photography and MA Photography course leader at The Cass Faculty of Art, Architecture and Design. She is a practicing photographer whose research interests include the family, home, perception and memory, focusing on the boundaries between public and private worlds. Her work has been published and exhibited widely, including at The International Incheon Women Artists' Biennale, The National Portrait Gallery, London and at The Geffrye Museum where she collaborated with visual anthropologist, Dr Inge Daniels. Andrews is a writer, curator and the research project director of The East End Archive at The Cass.

Nicholas Haeffner
Nicholas Haeffner is Senior Lecturer at The Cass, Faculty of Art Architecture and Design where he runs Critical and Contextual studies for art and photography students. He also teaches art history and theory on the MA in Curating the Contemporary which is run in partnership with the Whitechapel Gallery. He has published widely on film, photography, new media, critical theory and cultural history. He has written extensively on Alfred Hitchcock's films and has curated two Hitchcock related exhibitions. Haeffner is also a practicing photographer whose work has been featured in publications such as *The Independent*, *The Australian* and the *Griffith Review*.

THANKS

The authors would like to thank the following: Tamiko O'Brien, Anne Markey, Michael Upton, Mick Williamson, David George , Spencer Rowell, Adam Briggs, David Howells, Nicky Akehurst, The Building Exploratory, Amy Cooper-Wright, Andy Ganf, Hayley White, Kirsty Fife, Zelda Cheatle, Grace Gents Hair and all the photographers who gave permission for their work to be included.

AFTERWORD

ZELDA CHEATLE

There has been a recent surge of interest in how to tackle archiving of photographers work, a national campaign spearheaded by Jem Southam, Professor of Photography at Plymouth University who was spurred on by a fellow photographers untimely death and difficulty for the family trying to settle his estate. "So began an extended period of sporadic and uncoordinated enquiry. No photographer had thought the matter through and none had any idea of whom to turn for advice. When one considers how photography has flourished over the past four decades, and how much it has contributed to the cultural life of the country, this seems an appalling shame."

At The Cass, the dilemma has been resolved to a large extent by including work in direct relationship with the Archive, commissioned, exhibited, published or in research. The decision to acquire digital files rather than objects allows the Archive to grow and expand without facing major storage issues and is available, ultimately, online globally.

The open minds, the diversity and extended perceptions of the East End amongst staff at The Cass, their interpretation of exactly what the East End means or represents and the visual representation has inspired and enthused the most celebrated of East Enders, the most famous photographers. Combined with the knowledge and lengthy practice of many, The Cass East End Archive becomes synonymous with a new kind of digital archive. The very axis of its success is the combining of past with present and future.

The East End Archive can be viewed at www.eastendarchive.org.

Back cover:
Mick Williamson, from the *Photo-Diaries of Mick Williamson*, 1973–2013.

Black Dog Publishing Limited
10A Acton Street
London
WC1X 9NG
UK

t. +44 (0)207 713 5097
f. +44 (0)207 713 8682
e. info@blackdogonline.com
www.blackdogonline.com

Designed by Amy Cooper-Wright at Black Dog Publishing.

ISBN 978 1 908966 37 7

Archive: Imagining the East End is printed on sustainably sourced paper. Black Dog Publishing is an environmentally responsible company.

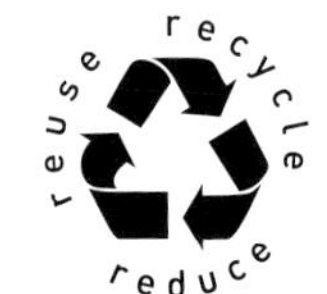

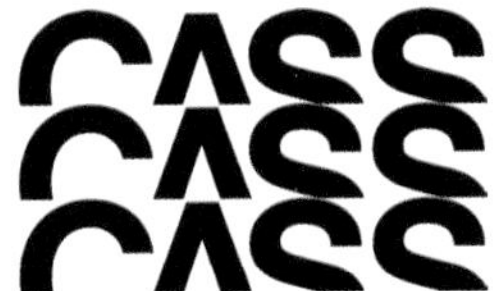

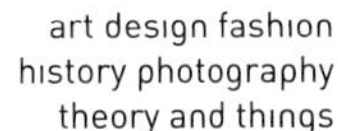

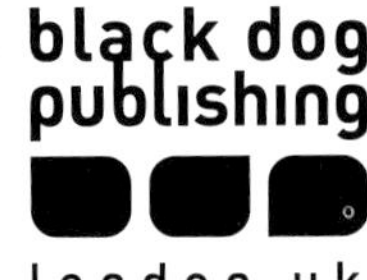

www.blackdogonline.com